# The Elementary School Library Makerspace

# The Elementary School Library Makerspace

## A Start-Up Guide

Marge Cox

LIBRARIES
UNLIMITED™

An Imprint of ABC-CLIO, LLC

Santa Barbara, California • Denver, Colorado

**Library of Congress Cataloging-in-Publication Data**
Names: Cox, Marge, author.
Title: The elementary school library makerspace : a start-up guide /
    Marge Cox.
Description: Santa Barbara, California : Libraries Unlimited, 2018. |
    Includes bibliographical references and index.
Identifiers: LCCN 2017052725 (print) | LCCN 2017036568 (ebook) |
    ISBN 9781440853395 (ebook) | ISBN 9781440853388 (alk. paper)
Subjects: LCSH: Makerspaces in libraries. | Elementary school libraries—
    Activity programs.
Classification: LCC Z716.37 (print) | LCC Z716.37 .C68 2018 (ebook) |
    DDC 025.5—dc23
LC record available at https://lccn.loc.gov/2017052725

ISBN: 978-1-4408-5338-8 (paperback)
       978-1-4408-5339-5 (ebook)

22  21  20  19  18    1  2  3  4  5

This book is also available as an eBook.

Libraries Unlimited
An Imprint of ABC-CLIO, LLC

ABC-CLIO, LLC
130 Cremona Drive, P.O. Box 1911
Santa Barbara, California 93116-1911
www.abc-clio.com

This book is printed on acid-free paper (∞)

Manufactured in the United States of America

To my husband, Jerry, and our wonderful children, Michelle and Greg, for their patience and understanding with my professional passion to make a difference in people's lives.

# Contents

# Preface

I love coming here! It is my favorite place at school.

—Fifth-grade male student

As an educator, words like these are music to my ears. What brings those kinds of comments from a child? A place that allows him or her to imagine, explore, and create—a Makerspace.

When I trained as a home economics teacher in the late 1960s, and early 1970s no one had heard of a Makerspace. Though certainly the excited students in my home economics classes showed that children loved creating. When I worked on my Master of Library Science in the 1980s, I learned a lot, but no one ever mentioned Makerspaces. Then in 2013, I read *School Library Makerspaces: Grades 6–12* by Leslie Preddy that introduced me to this 21st-century activity and my life has never been the same. I work in an elementary library, but the book had ideas I could adapt for my grade levels, too. On one hand, I shouldn't have been surprised, because I've known Leslie for years and she is always at the top of the educational game. Her book inspired me to start them in my elementary school library.

About that same time, I was awarded a small grant from our local educational foundation that let me buy some science materials for a specific project. When we finished with that project, it seemed a waste to store the materials until the content appeared the next school year. I put them out for students to use, when they finished choosing books. My Makerspaces were started!

From there, it has been an amazing adventure. We started with a few items laid out on tables in the library to seven Makerspaces supporting curriculum standards in the library plus another eight Makerspaces in an adjoining room to the library that is now named the Makerspace Lab. Students bring in their families when they visit school. Children choose to give up outdoor recess to come and create in the Makerspace Lab. Parents and grandparents attend the after-school-hours events and participate with their children and grandchildren.

Creating a space that provides hours of pleasure for so many people has been a source of great enjoyment. However, it has also been time consuming. As the popularity of Makerspaces has continued to grow, I reflected on my experience and thought I could help other Makerspace providers get their areas put together more quickly and easily than when I started mine.

This book provides readers with ten handouts for each content area. You can make a copy, add your standard at the bottom of the page, gather the materials, and you are good to go. The chapters give additional examples for each subject. You will have lots of ideas to use in your Makerspaces. Time is always the barrier to getting a new project started. This book will give you the solution to that concern, because it will save you hours. Don't let yourself be overwhelmed by the task. Take one step or Makerspace at a time and you'll be fine.

# Acknowledgments

Collaboration and a focus on what is best for youngsters are so much an important part of the education profession. I love the way people share their ideas and encourage one another. This book wouldn't have happened without many people exhibiting those behaviors.

Leslie Preddy's book, *School Library Makerspaces: Grades 6–12*, served as an inspiration to me in starting this new way to create excellent experiences for children in the library. Leslie's work exhibits the characteristics of excellence that we all strive to reach and I treasure our friendship of many years.

Most of my life was spent in Indiana and I am grateful for the treasure trove of media specialists, teachers, administrators, and professional organizations that helped me grow professionally and kept me laughing in the process. When I moved to Florida a few years ago, I wondered how I would develop deep personal, professional relationships again. Happily, the Florida Association for Media in Education and Southwest Florida Library Network provide great experiences. I've been blessed to work with another group of wonderful educators. Our Veterans Memorial Elementary (VME) School staff has a collective, collaborative heart that serves our students well. My principal, Dana Franklin Riashi, always encourages personal, and professional growth that provides opportunities to do what is best for our students. She has been an amazing advocate for our Makerspaces. Dr. Traci Kohler, Director of the Department of STEAM Resources, Instructional Technology and Media Services shows her commitment to Makerspaces by making them a key part of the professional development for media specialists. Dr. Kamela Patton, Collier County Public Schools superintendent, provides great leadership for STEAM and media specialists in many ways.

Our VME students and families have been the key to making our Makerspaces successful. I built them, but they had to come for the areas to be successful.

Jamie Brown has been a friend extraordinaire during this project. We first met when her sons were a part of the VME student body. She spent years being a volunteer in our library. I always treasured her skills, sweet ways with children and the ability to cut to the center of any issue and do all of that with a smile. However, little did I know when I started this book what a key encourager and help she would be for the completion of this project. I will be forever grateful to her!

Last but certainly not least, I appreciate the ABC-CLIO staff. My wonderful editor, Sharon Coatney, exhibited knowledge, patience, and professionalism. Project Editor, Emma Bailey, showed a wonderful willingness to work with me and help achieve my vision for this book. I appreciate their grace.

# Introduction

Creating Makerspaces can change your life. They bring nonreading students into the library who thought there might not be reason for them to visit. Makerspaces draw family members in, who might not have been in a school library since they were elementary school students. They let your frequent flyers have one more reason to love their favorite place on campus. In putting our Makerspaces together, I've learned some tips and tricks that will save you time, energy, and money.

## Starting and Maintaining

Every journey starts with the first step. Consider the big picture, but don't be overwhelmed by it. See what items are in your school's storage areas that could be repurposed for Makerspace use. Start with one that excites you and then create others as you have time.

As you develop new Makerspaces, you will want to take others apart. Plan how you want to store the materials. Decide if you want to stockpile items by content areas or months when you use them. You will probably need shelf and file cabinet areas. Label the containers and keep a spreadsheet of your disposable inventory. Records for items that are permanent can be placed in your library catalog system.

## Standards versus Exploration

Standards-based Makerspaces make it clear that the activity connects with instructional goals. Do children care about standards? Absolutely not. However, that information can make a difference to some adults. The Ideas to Get Started sheets in this book provide space at the bottom of the page for you to add your standards. I put mine there in smaller print. Then, it is available for any adult that finds that information necessary. The Ideas to Get Started sheets are suggestions for ways to use the materials, not requirements. Youngsters have the freedom to use materials as they choose.

Providing exploration Makerspaces just means the materials are set out without standards on the Ideas to Get Started sheets. Standards may not be considered that important in your school. If that is true, then you can use the sheets without adding the standards to them. The sheets help students get started with imaginative actions. Today's youngsters have not necessarily had experience with hands-on materials. When children first see Makerspaces, their first question may be, "What do I do with this?" The sheets can get them started.

## Budgeting and Buying

Some librarians don't have budgets, so starting something new can seem daunting. You really don't have to have a budget to start Makerspaces. Look around your school. You may be amazed at what you find. Let parents and community organizations know what you are starting. They may have items at home that you can use such as building toys their children have outgrown and items that can be recycled and used for building. Many civic organizations like to support students' projects. Apply for grants. You never know when you will be awarded one.

If you have access to funds, then before you make purchases think about how many different ways something may be used and by how many age groups. Consider if the item can be used to support different curriculum areas. You can have great Makerspaces without high-end, expensive electronics. You'll learn about specific examples as you read through the book.

## Collaboration

A part of what drew you to becoming a library media specialist was the pleasure of working with a variety of people. That characteristic will serve you well as you put together Makerspaces. Start with your administrators. They need to understand your vision so they can be advocates. Classroom teachers make great collaborators and their support can help get their students to the Makerspaces. Reach out to your PTO/A and community groups. Make contact with other schools, because their students could be mentors for your youngsters or they might be willing to help gather materials. Each person adds their special talents and skills to Makerspaces. Learn to delegate and value others' opinions. Things may not be done exactly as you would do them, but including lots of people allows for multiple viewpoints and spreads the good word about Makerspaces.

As you read this book, jot down names of people that you think would particularly enjoy a specific Makerspace. Talk with them how you could work together to make it happen in your school. Make notes about what works and what you would do differently when you do it again. Celebrate your successes and adapt those that didn't fly high the first time.

Think of this book as a collaborative tool. It has ideas that have worked for me. Read it, think about it, write in it, and share it with a friend. Use it in whatever way it helps you to create Makerspaces. We are all together in this educational adventure.

# CHAPTER 1

**History of Makerspaces**

Makerspaces are certainly a hot topic right now. They are not only in schools, but also in public libraries and community centers. You may wonder why so many people are interested in them. According to the *Dartmouth College Library Research Guide*, Makerspaces started in 2005 in Germany. However, the drive to make something that improves your life seems to be a part of human nature. People have been "makers" since early humans drew on the walls and made fire for cooking. At one point in our country's history, people made most of what they used or consumed. It was simply a way of life.

In more current times, schools tried to fill that basic need through "shop" or "home economics" classes, but those opportunities are scarce now. Arts classes have often been the victims of the cost cuts in school districts, too. Youngsters need a place to imagine, explore, and create. Makerspaces offer that opportunity.

Today the Do-It-Yourself movement impacts our lives. There are television shows that focus on home renovation. Websites abound where people have the opportunity to sell their handmade items worldwide. Stores that sell craft materials also offer how-to classes. People want the opportunity to make things.

Twenty-first-century technology offers possibilities that previous generations wouldn't have even imagined. 3D printers and robotic equipment are priced low enough that they are affordable for more and more people. Mobile phones include cameras that allow users to take videos and stills, and then edit them. Most homes have computers.

Makerspaces provide 21st-century creative minds a location and atmosphere to pursue their dreams. The drive to make something that improves your life has been a part of human nature for many generations and continues today in Makerspaces.

## Sources

A Brief History of Makerspaces. CuriosityCommons. https://curiositycommons.wordpress.com/a-brief-history-of-makerspaces/

Computer and Internet Use in the United States: 2013. Census Government. http://www.census.gov/content/dam/Census/library/publications/2014/acs/acs-28.pdf

Makerspaces: About. *Dartmouth College Library Research Guide*. http://researchguides.dartmouth.edu/makerspaces

# CHAPTER 2

## Why Do You Want to Create Makerspaces?

While it is good to know the history of Makerspaces, it is even more important to understand why you would put time and energy into creating them. Any new process or activity should be considered carefully and evaluated to see if it helps to achieve your school and library goals and mission. When you create Makerspaces based on your curriculum, you will find it easy to connect them to your goals and mission. They are one more tool to impact student achievement.

Here are three reasons why they are worth the time and effort to put in place in your school library.

1. They give school librarians an opportunity to show the breadth and depth of the school library and the collection, as well as affording an opportunity for them to display their professional leadership qualities.
2. They provide ways to connect curriculum in new formats.
3. They are good for students.

Let's look at each of the reasons a little more in depth. First, they give school librarians an opportunity to show the breadth and depth of the library and the collection, as well as provide an opportunity for them to display their professional leadership qualities. Today's facilities and collections are a far cry from those of bygone years. The parents of your students may not have been in a school library since they were a child and have no idea about a 21st-century facility and program. They may be surprised to learn not only about the technology available, but also the quality of children's and young adult literature. Today's depth of information about STEAM (Science, Technology, Engineering, Arts and Math) astounds most people.

Even many new teachers don't know the possibilities that abound for them and their students in today's school library. You will likely be the first person to introduce many adults to the world of 21st-century school libraries.

For students who don't see themselves as avid readers, Makerspaces give them other reasons to visit the school library. They need to know this is a place for hands-on learners to shine. Providing a Makerspace will draw more students into the facility and then give them reasons to explore the print collection. As you make materials available for the Makerspaces include books that show models or examine additional ideas about the topics. As students complete projects, sharing their work online places it in the 21st-century culture of posting interests for others to see. Many people have no idea that today's school libraries contain video production facilities and equipment, so when students create and post products, it shows the options available for today's library users.

Twenty-first century school libraries need to not only reflect society, but lead the way for students to have opportunities in experimenting with and learning new skills.

Makerspaces are also a way to show your professional leadership qualities. You are modeling what you ask your students to do, which is to learn new information and incorporate it into your life. You are exploring innovative options and sharing them with others. You don't have to know how to use every possibility for each piece of material that you provide. You just need to provide a safe environment for students to explore.

Second, Makerspaces provide occasions to connect curriculum in new ways. Research tells us that hands-on activities engage students (Kurti, Kurti, and Fleming 2014). Makerspaces are the ultimate applied experience. They allow youngsters to experiment with ideas and supplies. Some of the supplies will be materials that they have at home and they can recreate the activity there. However, other items will give children the chance to use materials that they wouldn't have access to normally. It helps to level the playing field, so that all children have access to quality experiences.

We also know from research that companies want their workers to be able to work comfortably with others, as well as alone (Adams, 2014). To do that as adults, they need to have collaborative experiences as children. When using Makerspaces, children get a chance to work alone and in small groups, depending upon the project. They get experiences in resolving disagreements and the joy of achievement when a project is completed.

When they can physically engage with materials, the textbook theories become real to them. For example, a fraction is just a set of numbers, until you cut fruit into specifically sized pieces to make fruit salad. Then you understand what a half of something looks like once you have divided it from the whole. You have met a health standard of learning about nutritious food, as well as a math standard concerning fractions. When students put circuits together to produce a light or sound, they understand how important connections are to achieve a product's outcome and science becomes applicable to their lives.

Makerspaces make a great format to work collaboratively with teachers to meet curriculum standards. Teachers aren't likely to have Makerspaces set up in their classrooms, but they will thoroughly enjoy their students using one. The old saying that "many hands make light work" shows to be true when it comes to Makerspaces. Creating a Makerspace in the library makes it available to all the students in the school. Encourage teachers to let their students use it by teaching in it, creating opportunities for youngsters to visit and connecting to curriculum. Those curriculum connections make it clear that we are critical to student achievement, not an extra. Your Makerspace shows that school librarians bring special opportunities to staff and students.

The last reason to create Makerspaces is perhaps the most important one—they are good for students. Whenever a new idea comes into the educational realm, my plumb line before I get involved is always, "Is it good for children?" Too many ideas are put in place, because they are convenient for adults. Makerspaces absolutely provide wonderful opportunities for today's learners. The current emphasis on testing creates a lot of stress to students, their families, and staff.

Makerspaces provide the chance to imagine, create, explore, and learn without strain. Imagine being a youngster who finishes a test and then gets to go to the Makerspace Lab to build a magnetic structure. Maybe a student is trying to understand the important people in history. He or she gets to go the Makerspace Lab and make a baseball card-style project about a person of his or her choice. If teachers are still requiring book reports, suggest that students share about their books by making a book trailer and it gets posted for other students to see.

Makerspaces also provide a wonderful opportunity to involve families in the library. As parents visit the facility, they can participate with the hands-on activities. Providing after-school or evening experiences where parents and children can participate together gives new reasons to visit and be involved in your program. At our school, the expectation is one adult for each child who attends the one hour after school-hour sessions. Parents have commented on how much they enjoyed focused on spending quality time with one child. The children love sharing the experience with their parents. We've also had some grandparents participate, who made it clear that they were wowed by the quality of the time together and activities that they participated in.

So when thinking about the reasons why you would create Makerspaces, consider these ideas. Will there be some work to putting together Makerspaces? Absolutely! Are they worth it? You bet! They provide the opportunity for school librarians to show the breadth and depth of the library and collection, make curriculum connections and they are good for students in multiple ways. Begin the adventure today!

## References

Adams, Susan. "The 10 Skills Employers Most Want in 2015 Graduates," *Forbes,* November 12, 2014. http://www.forbes.com/sites/susanadams/2014/11/12/the-10-skills-employers-most-want-in-2015-graduates/#5fa3a2c019f6

Kurti, R. Steven, Deborah Kurti, and Laura Fleming. "The Environment and Tools of Great Makerspaces," Part 2, *Teacher Librarian,* October 2014, pp. 8–12.

# CHAPTER 3

## Curriculum Connections Overview

You want the Makerspaces to interest all the grades that your school serves. When I first started them, I worried that the activities wouldn't span our pre-K–5 grades academic and interest levels. However, what I have found is that each student uses the Makerspaces appropriately for their abilities. What continually amazes me is how they utilize materials not only in the ways that I envisioned, but then go far beyond any of my expectations. Even with specific curriculum standards and suggested ideas, their creativity flourishes.

Anything that I want to accomplish, I have to put in my calendar, or it doesn't happen. I find that it is true for Makerspaces, too. I look at my calendar and see when I can look at our curriculum guides, plan, and get the materials out for the Makerspaces. I change mine monthly, but that is a self-imposed guideline. You may choose to change them every six or nine weeks. You need to set up a schedule that works for you and fits in with your other responsibilities. You certainly can just put materials out and see what the students do with them.

There is one philosophy of Makerspaces that says they should all be exploratory. However, you may get more teacher and administration buy-in, if you tie at least some of them to curriculum standards. I try to incorporate standards-based as well as exploration Makerspaces each month. The ones in our media center have standards with them. However, students have the freedom to use the materials they choose. The ones in our Makerspace Lab are exploratory stations. Any time I'm doing direct instruction with the Makerspace materials, the activity is standards-based, the same as any other instruction that I do.

To meet curriculum connections, look carefully at your district's curriculum guide to see which of the standards lend themselves to hands-on activities. If your state uses Common Core, then explore http://www.corestandards.org. This should have the latest information about those standards. Also, visit the national associations that concentrate on that content area.

When I begin creating Makerspaces, I check our district curriculum guides and look for the big ideas as well as the standards for the coming month. I choose different grade levels for different topics. For example, one month I may look at second grade for social studies, fifth grade for math, third grade for science, and fourth grade for English/language arts. The next month, I choose different grade levels for each content area. Some of the concepts spiral throughout the grade levels. Then, I choose a specific standard and think about a hands-on activity that will give the children a deeper understanding of the content. After that, I look at the materials I have available. I create an "Ideas to Consider" sheet. The top of the sheet could include pictures of books or materials, but it doesn't have to have any graphics. Next comes directions that could be used for a project. The bottom includes standards. The sheets in this book have that segment blank so that you can add your specific standards. You could use small font, because they really are for adults who want to know if the activity is standards-based. Students don't care about standards. When that is done, you are ready to get the materials out. Choose a content area that you are most comfortable with to start and then expand to additional content areas as your comfort level rises.

Decide where to put the materials and your "Ideas to Consider" sheet. Voila! You and your students are ready for exciting new adventures.

# CHAPTER 4

## Science Makerspace Ideas

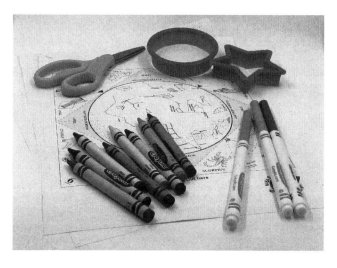

Science incorporates so many concepts that you are sure to interest youngsters with at least one of them. The examples given below are some of the concepts students enjoy.

NASA offers wonderful activities about stars and constellations that students thoroughly enjoyed when their science units were about space. Make copies of the constellation sheets, and put out scissors (because there is cutting involved) and books about the solar system. The NASA information explains that stars aren't really "star-shaped" and vary in size and color, depending upon their heat. Participants cut and fold the constellation sheets to see what star formations to look for in the night sky for that month. Another choice is to use the cookie cutters, pencils, and scissors to make stars. There are crayons available to color them in colors appropriate for a variety of temperatures. With either project, students walk out of the media center with their individual constellation example or sample stars.

The science activities listed here encourage students to use microscopes. Set a microscope out with different items for the students to look at through the device. Try some nature items such as rocks or leaves as well as manmade things such as paper or fabric. Ask them to draw what they see with the natural eye and how it looks differently through the microscope. The level of detail in the pictures drawn with the usual eyesight is clearly different than the ones showing the microscopic perspective. Youngsters quickly see that the microscope changes the way we see things. The standard is met and each participant has a personalized piece of artwork that represents the experience.

Magnetism fascinates children when they study it. There are several companies that produce magnetized pieces with which to build any number of items. Students love the opportunity to create structures with them, but plain magnets provide hours of exploration, too. Our Magnet Makerspace allows students to explore with magnets and other materials to see how they work together and what happens if there is a material between the two magnets. They certainly can write their responses, but recording a video provides a great opportunity to capture their enthusiasm.

The Rock Makerspace blends science, language arts, and technology standards. Students choose a rock from several options and then describe it using at least three adjectives. They take a picture of it and their card. If you have an electronic place to post student work, great! If not, print and post them in the media center. If your space allows for it, you could display the cards, close to the 550 Dewey Decimal System of your library.

Matter is a science concept that children sometimes struggle to understand. However, when you connect an activity that they already love, such as blowing bubbles to the educational mix, the idea starts to make sense. This Makerspace includes bottles of bubble mixture and wands for them to enjoy. Also include an "Ideas to Try" sheet that says when you add your breath (a gas) to the bubble solution (a liquid), you have used two types of matter. You can buy the bubble mixtures, but there are numerous websites that give recipes to make your own. Making the solution could be a great activity for student media assistants.

Food chains are a standard in many science curriculums, but children sometimes have difficulty understanding the idea. To help students better comprehend that concept, they create a food chain with strips of colored paper. They label each strip with one step of a food chain and then staple or tape the ends together to make an appropriate chain. Students can take their creations or leave it in the library for display. Whichever they choose to do, they understand the concept more completely, because they have created something concrete.

Simple machines can be so much fun to make and operate. This Makerspace provides a plethora of materials for students to use in creating simple machines. Sample books from the 621.8 section are there to give students inspiration, but they are only limited by their imagination. Connect to their visual arts and language arts skills by writing a story about their creation(s). Keep notebooks in the media center so they can place their work in them, so others can see and enjoy it.

Sound variations make for an interesting Makerspace activity. Again, students will integrate science and language arts. If you have a high tolerance for noise, include your music standards. Several items are put out and students explore the sounds they can make. Of course, they can always experiment with using their normal inside voice and a whispering tone. They describe the sounds with expressive adjectives and then record the sounds and their descriptive terms.

Learning the five senses of sight, sound, touch, taste, and smell is a concept included in science instruction. Set out pictures of the appropriate body parts and signs of the senses and have students match them. A more individualized activity is for students to draw their own picture of the body part and label it with the name of the body part and which sense is connected with it. Include signs of the five senses words, so their spelling will be correct. Another option is to put out a variety of objects and have them draw and label which sense they use to describe one of the items.

Thinking about Earth's place in the universe provides several opportunities for students to experience hands-on opportunities. This activity will take several days, but gives a chance to show how Makerspaces can be used in direct instruction. NASA provides a couple of sites that are helpful to your students:

✦ https://www.nasa.gov/content/planets-moons-and-dwarf-planets

✦ https://www.nasa.gov/audience/forstudents/index.html

Choose a type of papier-mâché mix that best fits your needs and budget. There are several choices on the Internet. Blow up the balloons and have children attach newspaper strips to the balloons with some variation of glue, paste, or papier-mâché. Let it dry at least overnight. Using a globe as a model, students paint "their planet" with appropriate colors or have different students make different planets. If all of them make an Earth, great. If they make a variety of planets, then label them and hang them in the correct order from the sun. Display their written research with the model.

For additional science ideas, look at the following websites:

**Education.Com**—http://www.education.com/science-fair/
This site breaks science into six areas. It also categorizes ideas by kindergarten, elementary, middle, and high school. You can easily adjust the science fair ideas to Makerspaces.

**National Aeronautics and Space Administration**—https://www.nasa.gov
You will love the wealth of information here. Click on the Education button to get started. Peruse the educators, students, and NASA Kids club tabs.

**National Science Teachers Association**—https://www.nsta.org
This is the professional organization for science teachers. You can find the latest Science standards posted here. The classroom resources are also helpful. Each year, they release a list of Outstanding Science Trade Books for Students K–12. Those books make a great start to expanding your science collection with quality books.

**Science Buddies**—http://www.sciencebuddies.org/science-fair-projects/teacher_resources .shtml
You will find tabs for students and parents, as well as teachers to be helpful. If you use Google classroom, it is especially easy to create assignments from this site. You can adjust the ideas to Makerspaces.

# Ideas for Getting Started

## SCIENCE
### Stars

1. Look in the 520 section of our library for a book about stars.

2. Write one interesting fact that you found and put the title of the book on your paper.

3. NASA also has information about stars.

4. Make a Star Finder from spaceplace.nasa.gov/starfinder/en/ and use it with a friend.

5. This evening, look at the night sky. Tomorrow record what you have learned about stars.

Create!

# Ideas for Getting Started

## SCIENCE
### Microscopes

1. Take a look at one or two items through the microscope.

2. Draw a picture of what one of the items looks like when you look at it with your natural eyesight. Draw a second picture of the same item when you view it through the microscope.

3. Post your pictures on the bulletin board.

# Ideas for Getting Started

## SCIENCE
### Food Chains

1. Choose an appropriate book from the 574.53 section about food chains.

2. Take three links and label each one with a step of the food chain.

3. Use links to make a chain.

4. Draw an illustration of your food chain in the real world.

Create!

# Ideas for Getting Started

### SCIENCE
### Magnets

1. Look in the 530 section of our library for books about magnetism.

2. Write one interesting fact that you found and put the title of the book on your paper.

3. Experiment with the magnets.

4. Write or record how it feels to put them together and take them apart.

5. What is one place you see magnets at work in the real world?

Create!

# Ideas for Getting Started

## SCIENCE
### Rocks

1. Pick up one of the rocks and carefully look at it.

2. On one of the index cards, write your name, the rock's name and draw a picture of it.

3. List three adjectives to describe it.

4. Take a picture of the rock and your card.

5. Look in the 550 section of our library to find books about rocks.

Create!

# Ideas for Getting Started

## SCIENCE
### Matter

1. Carefully pick up the bottle of liquid bubbles.

2. Take the wand out of the jar and blow through it. You are adding gas to the liquid and creating a bubble.

3. Look at a book from the 530.4 section of our library.

4. Draw or record another time that you have seen different states of matter.

# Ideas for Getting Started

## SCIENCE
## Simple Machines

1. Choose one of the books from the 621.8 section of our library to get ideas.

2. Using the materials that are on the table, explore how to put them together to make a simple machine.

3. Write and illustrate a story that includes simple machines.

4. Add your work to the Library Original Work Notebook.

# Ideas for Getting Started

## SCIENCE
## Sound

1. Using the materials on the table, explore with them to make several different sounds.

2. Describe the sounds with expressive adjectives.

3. Use the iPad to capture the sounds you have made and how you describe them.

4. To learn more about sound, go to the 534 section of our library.

# Ideas for Getting Started

## SCIENCE
### 5 Senses

1. Think about your 5 senses and which body part connects with them. For example, your eyes see, your ears heard, your tongue tastes, your nose smells, and your skin feels touches.

2. Using at least one of the 5 senses, describe any of the objects on the table and label which sense and body part you used to get your information.

3. Post your picture with the labels.

4. Find books about the senses in the 612.8 section of the library.

# Ideas for Getting Started

## SCIENCE
## Solar System

1. Take a look at one of the following websites: www.nasa.gov/content/planets-moons-and-dwarf-planets or www.nasa.gov/audience/forstudents/index.html

2. Choose a planet to research by asking at least one question about the planet.

3. Blow up a balloon and paper-mache it.

4. When it is dry, paint it appropriate colors.

5. Display the answer to your question with the model.

# CHAPTER 5

**Technology Makerspace Ideas**

While today's students often have technology in their hands, they still need to see ways to use it in educationally appropriate ways. Open the doors for them to see educational technology as exciting and fun by creating some of these Makerspaces.

Technology encompasses a wide array of possibilities. It will depend on what you have available in your district, as to what your best choices are for this Makerspace. If you have encyclopedia software available for your school, start with that. The packages that the students use for research oftentimes have activity areas, too. Those parts may never get used, if you don't point them out and encourage students to use them. They will be a better use of online game time, than what the students find randomly on the Internet. Youngsters will start to see that the software can be fun as well as educational.

If you think of research as a way to answer questions, then those sites give students a chance to do personal fact finding. Use either a laptop or tablet and set it to one of the research options that you have available. Let students choose a topic that they are interested in. Have them write one fact that they learned. Post the facts on a bulletin board. Children love to have their work displayed.

Padlet (https://padlet.com/my/dashboard) provides a free way to post your students' work electronically. Make a Padlet to get them started. Consider starting one where your students post about their favorite book from your state's book list. Once you have created that Padlet, take a look at your curriculum maps and look for other content that lends itself to students sharing their points of view. That could include multiple ways to solve a math problem, reasons why the early settlers wanted to move to West, or examples of habitats.

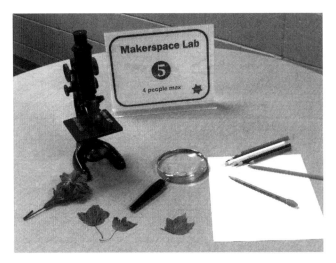

QR Codes let you connect a code to an item that refers to another item or website. Start by creating a QR code. One site that creates QR codes is http://www.qr-code-generator.com. Check the Internet to find a QR Reader to utilize the codes. Students can connect a book to the author's website. They can make a website about a book and connect the two. They could connect a map to book. Many students have phones and QR Codes give them another way to use the devices in an educational format.

Remember that technology tools don't have to be just computers. Numerous tools can be used. Pull out the microscopes and magnifying glasses. When the science curriculum focuses on plants, place leaves and flowers on the table with the microscope and magnifying glass tools. Have students make drawings of what they see with their natural eyesight and what they see using one of the tools. Their artwork can be displayed or they can take it with them, if they so choose.

Consider cameras. Many students have phones and use cameras on a regular basis. However, they don't often use them for educational projects. Introduce them to storyboards as a tool to plan their pictures and videos for projects. Videos and photos can be put together to make book trailers, provide visual explanations for nonfiction projects, or illustrations for stories. Once children understand the process to put videos and photos together, they will see numerous ways to use those skills.

One of the newer technology tools, virtual reality glasses, opens innovative possibilities for Makerspace users. Using them gives a new perspective to life. Children can utilize their language arts skills and write about what they see. Another option for the glasses is to have youngsters write about what could happen next or draw the scene they think would follow. Their work could be recorded for sharing with others.

You may have electronic readers that aren't used as much as when you first bought them. They can have a new life in Makerspaces. Have the students read the selections on the device and then use other tools to create a 30-second booktalk about one of the stories from the e-reader. Watch the circulation of the eBooks rise, when students get excited about the stories that they hold.

Basic coding opportunities appear in many elementary schools now. You could purchase a Raspberry Pi (https://www.raspberrypi.org) and have students work with it, but it isn't the only option. Include coding books in your collection. Take a look at the Code.org website (https://code.org/educate/curriculum/elementary-school). Another site to investigate is Tynker (https://www.tynker.com). Kodable provides opportunities as well (https://www.kodable.com).

Does your school have a student studio where you produce daily announcements? If so, that is a ready-made Makerspace. It is too much equipment to only be used for a few minutes a

day. Small groups of students will love using it, instead of going to recess. You can use it when you want to capture student projects to share with others. Train a few students to be "directors" or "producers" and they can assist others with their productions.

If you have funds for printers and scanners, include them in your Makerspace. Students love having access to those technology tools. They provide opportunities that students may not have opportunity to use at home. Students find 3D printers particularly interesting and they now come in a range of prices. They are nice to have, but certainly not essential to your Technology Makerspace.

As you look to start or expand your technology Makerspace, be content to start small. Plan larger purchases into your budget, look for funding from PTO/A or apply for grants. You can do a lot with a little.

If your state has technology standards, use them. If it doesn't, then take a look at the following sites.

**American Association of School Librarians**—http://www.ala.org/aasl/standards/
You can download the standards directly from the site. While they don't include the word, "technology," you certainly need to follow these standards when creating or using technology.

**Association for Educational Communications and Technology**—http://aect.site-ym
.com/?page=about_landing
You find some helpful publications here and conferences that you would enjoy.

**Education World**—http://www.educationworld.com/standards/national/technology/k_12
.shtml
This site divides the tech standards into six areas and gives details for each one.

**International Society of Technology Educators**—http://www.iste.org/standards/standards/
for-students-2016
These standards are divided into seven areas. The site provides a great deal of detail about each one.

# Ideas for Getting Started

## TECHNOLOGY
## Online Encyclopedia

1.  Think about a question that you have about any topic.

2.  Use this software to find an interesting fact about your question.

3.  Share your fact with others by writing it on a card.

4.  Add an illustration to your fact.

5.  Post the card with your illustration on the Makerspace bulletin board.

# Ideas for Getting Started

## TECHNOLOGY
## Padlet

1. Go to https://padlet.com/my/ dashboard.

2. To add your ideas, click on the plus sign.

3. Type your first name and last initial to identify yourself as the person posting.

4. Type the title of your favorite state award book.

5. Type at least one sentence about why it is your favorite.

Create!

# Ideas for Getting Started

## TECHNOLOGY
## QR Codes

1.  Consider when it would be helpful to connect two pieces of information. For example, if you are working on research about states or countries, you can connect tourism sites to your research project.

2.  Use http://www.qr-code-generator.com to make a QR code.

3.  Connect the QR code to the appropriate item.

4.  Download a QR reader. Use your phone or tablet to double check that the QR code works.

Create!

From *The Elementary School Library Makerspace: A Start-Up Guide* by Marge Cox. Santa Barbara, CA: Libraries Unlimited. Copyright © 2018.

# Ideas for Getting Started

## TECHNOLOGY
### Magnifying Glasses—Microscopes

1. Draw a picture of what one of the items look like when you view it with your natural eyesight.

2. Use the magnifying glasses or microscope to look at the same item on the table.

3. Draw a picture of what the item looks like using a tool.

4. Feel free to take your artwork with you; but, if you choose, you may post it.

# Ideas for Getting Started

## TECHNOLOGY
### Cameras

1. Use the storyboard sheets to write the basics of your project.

2. Take the photos that you planned in your storyboard.

3. Record the videos that you planned in your storyboard.

4. Finalize your project by putting the segments together

5. Post it on the library channel for others to see.

# Ideas for Getting Started

## TECHNOLOGY
## Virtual Reality Glasses

1. Take a look at one of the options available on the glasses.

2. Imagine what you think would be a good panel to appear next.

3. Write a script that includes at least two people speaking.

4. Create an illustration that supports your writing.

5. Record your script and your artwork. Be sure to give credit to the additional person in your video.

Create!

# Ideas for Getting Started

## TECHNOLOGY
### Electronic Readers

1. Scan the titles on the e-readers.

2. Choose one of the stories to read.

3. After you finish the story, write a 30-second commercial to encourage others to read the selection.

4. Record your ideas. Be sure to include the title, author, and genre. Be specific about why you liked the story.

5. Post it on the school channel.

# Ideas for Getting Started

## TECHNOLOGY
### Coding

1. You will find coding books in the 004 and 005 sections of our library. Choose at least one of them to read.

2. Take a look at the coding website: https://www.commonsense.org/education/top-picks/best-coding-tools-for-elementary.

3. Choose one of the options and experiment with creating a code.

4. Record why and how you wrote the code. Also, tell what you would do differently the next time.

Create!

# Ideas for Getting Started

## TECHNOLOGY
### Studio

1. Look at the variety of studio equipment available for you to use.

2. Consider what type of product will best allow you to get your idea across to the audience: i.e. video, poster, interview, etc.

3. Sign up for the equipment that you need to use to produce your project.

4. Produce your project. Share it on line or on the library channel.

# Ideas for Getting Started

## TECHNOLOGY
### Printers and Scanners

1. Think about the tech projects you want to produce. A printer could be used to create pages of a book. A scanner allows you to put several different items on the screen to make a collage.

2. Choose whether a printer or scanner will help you create a great final project to share your ideas with others.

3. Create a timeline so you can accomplish making your project.

4. Use the printer and/or scanner. Be sure to turn it off when you are finished.

Create!

# CHAPTER 6

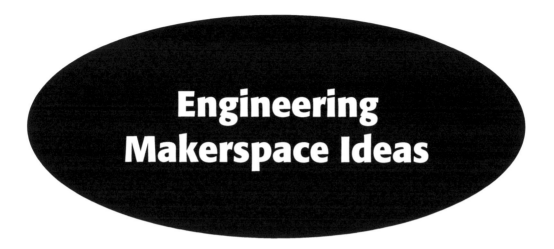

## Engineering Makerspace Ideas

An engineering curriculum is not commonplace in elementary schools. I once heard a person who had graduated from college with a degree in engineering, say "it is just about processes and systems." When you think about it in those terms you can see how to make a connection for children.

When I started our Makerspaces, engineering was the one that most concerned me about appealing to students. I shouldn't have worried. It is one of their favorites. Utilize a variety of building tools and they will use all of them with vim and vigor. You may find that your print engineering collection is a little skimpy, but once you start to specifically look for engineering-focused books, you will find that a lot of great options are available today. With the emphasis on STEM, there are so many more choices available now, than once existed. This is a Makerspace where you will be able to use second-hand items, too. As families outgrow building material toys they will be glad to share, if they know you are interested. The one parameter that we put in place for this Makerspace is that student-created products must be positive creations such as bridges, homes, vehicles, etc. Weapons making is not an option.

While candy is not something you may normally keep in the library for a treat, it can be useful in Makerspaces. Toothpicks, marshmallows, and gumdrops make interesting structures. Talk to the students about how the materials are handled by lots of people and they wouldn't want to eat them. However, they will create some amazing structures with it.

There are several different sets of colorful magnetic building sets out now. Children love the pull of the magnetized pieces. They provide the opportunity to talk about magnets and how they work, as well as structural design. The different shapes allow for children to experiment with a wide variety of possible designs.

Blocks have been around for many years, but today's youngsters have many choices that previous generations of children could not enjoy. Look for wooden and plastic blocks. Some students prefer the texture of one to another. Then look for sets with a variety of sizes and shapes. Encourage your young builders to see how building skills can be used by including books in your collection that show a variety of building structures.

Earlier generations of children enjoyed TinkerToys. Plastic straws provide a current adaptation that can be lots of fun. The bright colors draw attention to the designs and give a sense of excitement to the construction team. As you choose materials, you want some that are inexpensive and easily replaceable. Straws fit the bill. You can use play-dough to make connectors. An advantage of straws over wooden sticks is that that they can bend. Arches give an interesting look to student-created construction.

Simple machines are a part of some science curriculums, but they make great tools for a Makerspace, too. Provide students with pieces and parts that can be put together in a variety of ways. Putting out pictures of some simple machines will inspire children to manipulate the tools on the table in ways to create interesting machines. Tie in language arts standards by having students write about what they have created.

Many children make simple paper airplanes, but put that concept in a Makerspace and you will see more unique creations. Set out paper, paperclips, crayons, markers, and scissors and you will be amazed at what the young flight designers create. This could be a great time to make a social studies connection. Place some pictures of previously named planes in the Makerspace. Those pictures can include captions that give information about the aircraft and how they were important in history. The students will have a blast flying their contraptions. However, do remind them of "appropriate airspace." Designate a section of the library to be an airport, and remind the students to not fly the planes on the school bus.

Young children may not understand how gears work, until we provide a hands-on experience for them. Gear sets can be purchased in a variety of sizes and colors now. Children love to make things move and will figure out lots of different ways to put the gears together. Forewarning—gears tend to be noisy. A part of the Makerspace should include videos of gears being used, so that children see them in action.

People of all ages love to play with play-dough. Using it in an Engineering Makerspace gives the long-loved substance a whole new set of possibilities. Of course, there will be play-dough there, but also include tongue depressors, tiny dowel rods, small pieces of cardboard, beads, and pieces of tin foil. They can be utilized to build any number of items. Makers can use their newly created building in their own writing. Combining the language arts standards that focus on setting with this Makerspace can help young authors to understand story setting as location.

If you're putting your Makerspaces together on a shoestring budget, then this one will be easy to put in place. Buy paper cups and index cards. Children can build cup and card towers collaboratively or competitively. You could tie them to a children's book, such as *Rapunzel* or *The Man Who Walked between the Towers*. The towers could also be tied to math standards that deal with basic shapes. For example, give directions that say to build a tower that contains nine triangles or three layers.

Bridges are amazing architectural creations. Let children experience some of that beauty when they build them. This Makerspace is only limited by your imagination. You can use straws, dowel rods, building blocks, or anything else in your supply cabinet. Take a look in your print collection for books about bridges. If you don't have good books about bridges, there are some great choices out there now for purchase. Set the books up in the Makerspace along with a variety of materials for building. Children know the purpose of bridges, but they may not know how they are constructed. A few minutes in this space will give them the beginnings of understanding construction.

Engineering can take so many forms. Even for elementary children, there are a myriad of opportunities to enjoy it. Take a look at these websites to get additional engineering ideas.

**American Society for Engineering Education**—http://www.asee.org
This organization hosts blogs, newsletters, and conferences about engineering.

**Engineering is Elementary**—http://www.eie.org
The Museum of Science in Boston hosts this site, which provides curriculum for first- to eighth-grade students.

**Standards for K–12 Engineering Education**—http://teachingcommons.cdl.edu/ngss/engineering_design/documents/pdf_000.pdf
This site includes not only standards, but also arguments for and against having engineering standards.

**Teach Engineering**—https://www.teachengineering.org
These engineering standards are aligned to Common Core science and math standards.

# Ideas for Getting Started

## ENGINEERING
## Candy and Toothpick Structures

1. Remember that all the candy has been handled by lots of people, so you won't want to eat it.

2. Sketch a design that you would like to build.

3. Take a careful look at the assorted gumdrops, marshmallows, gummies, etc.

4. Experiment with different materials to create your design.

5. Take a picture of your final creation and post it on the Makerspace board.

Create!

# Ideas for Getting Started

## ENGINEERING
## Magnetic Building Sets

1. Use several different shapes and sizes of pieces.  See how tall of a tower you can build.

2. Can you make the pieces go over the side of the table and travel to the floor, while staying linked together?

3. Give your creation a name.  Use the cards at the table to make a nametag for your product.

4. Take a picture of your final creation and post it on the Makerspace board.

Create!

# Ideas for Getting Started

## ENGINEERING
### Block Sets

1. Browse through the books from the 720 section to get ideas about different styles of architecture.

2. Look at the blocks to see which ones could provide you the tools to build a housing structure.

3. Develop a building.

4. Make a recording that includes the title of the book that inspired your structure, a name for what you built, and where you would locate it.

# Ideas for Getting Started

## ENGINEERING
## Plastic Straws

1. Notice the different sizes of straws on the table.

2. Imagine what you could build with them.

3. Experiment with putting some of them together using the play-dough.

4. Consider the different items you could build such as furniture or modes of transportation.

5. Take a picture of your creation and write about it.

Create!

# Ideas for Getting Started

## ENGINEERING
## Simple Machines

1. Take a look at the books on the table from the 621.8 or 745.5 sections. They show pictures of simple machines.

2. After making a few simple machines, try to make more elaborate ones.

3. Design a machine that you don't believe exists, but you think should be a part of our world.

4. Write about your new creation and post it in the Makerspace Notebook.

Create!

# Ideas for Getting Started

## ENGINEERING
## Paper Airplanes

1. Look at the books on the table from the 745.59 section. Notice the different plane shapes and their names.

2. Choose one of the patterns and use it to make an airplane.

3. Decorate it however you choose.

4. Fly your plane at "The Landing Strip." When you leave here, keep it in your book bag until you reach home.

Create!

From *The Elementary School Library Makerspace: A Start-Up Guide* by Marge Cox. Santa Barbara, CA: Libraries Unlimited. Copyright © 2018.

# Ideas for Getting Started

## ENGINEERING
### Gears

1. Take a look at the books from the 621.8 section on the table. They will show gears at work.

2. Using some of the pieces on the table, put them together so that they make each other turn.

3. Experiment with creating gears that are tall, as well as those that stay flat.

4. Draw a picture of your favorite gear set and state what you would have it move.

Create!

# Ideas for Getting Started

## ENGINEERING
## Play-Dough

1. Draw a design of a building that you would like to build.

2. Choose any of the materials on the table to build and decorate it.

3. Write a short story with your building as an important part of the story.

4. Record what you've written. Show your building in the recording.

# Ideas for Getting Started

## ENGINEERING
## Cups and Cards

1. Think about the towers you have seen in real life or in literature. For example, you might have seen the water tower in your area or read *Rapunzel* or *The Man Who Walked Between the Towers*.

2. Practice building a small tower with the cups and cards.

3. Ask a friend to build a tower with you.

4. Challenge a friend to see who can build the tallest tower in a set amount of time.

Create!

# Ideas for Getting Started

## ENGINEERING
### Bridges

1. As you look at the books on the table, from the 624 section, pay attention to the different shapes and sizes of the bridges.

2. Choose some of the materials on the table to build a bridge.

3. Give your bridge a name.

4. Record a one-minute video about your bridge. Include the most difficult part of building the bridge and what would you do differently the next time.

Create!

# CHAPTER 7

## Arts Makerspace Ideas

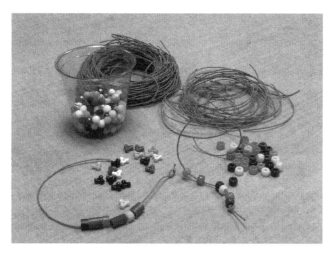

That is arts with an "s," because the Makerspaces need to include a variety of arts, not just visual art. Check with your local art and music teachers to see what they use for standards, if you don't see any in your school district's curriculum guide. You may not have done a lot with the arts in the school library previously, but these Makerspaces give students a new vibe for the library. Enjoy the chance to spread your educational wings and try new things.

A fun first art Makerspace is making bracelets with the cheapest beads you can find or make and hemp string. Watch for sales to provide large quantities of beads or make them with drying clay. There are recipes on the Internet, if you want your students to make their own clay. You can also connect to math standards that focus on patterns. Put out books about making jewelry along with the materials so they can see other jewelry making opportunities. The boys love this creative opportunity, as much as the girls.

Origami, the art of paper folding, can be enjoyed by all ages. You'll need to provide paper and directions. There are lots of books with directions, but you will also find support by searching the Internet and looking at video postings. Seeing finished work can really help youngsters to better visualize what they are trying to accomplish. Depending upon the age of the children in your school, a literature connection could be *Sadako and the 1000 Paper Cranes*. If you would like a more light-hearted type of connecting literature, try *Lissy's Friends* or *The Pirate's Girl's Treasure*. Of course, you can connect to math standards with the measuring needed to create origami.

Students love to perform plays! If you have stuffed animals or puppets in your library as reading buddies, here is a new way to use them. This can blend with language arts standards of writing, if the students create their own scripts. If they choose to use an already created script, the language arts standards of speaking and listening can still be met through this Makerspace. If you have a small stage area in the library, it would be the perfect place to have the plays. If not, just make a stage area by rearranging furniture to create a small area for an audience. Students could make advertising flyers or commercials to let others know about it. If you have Reader's Theater Scripts, they can be another source to share with your young actors.

Children love to use tools. Makerspaces provide a space to use tools that they may not have access to at home. For example, you can provide them a special experience with a sewing machine. At one time, that tool would have been in most homes or there were home economics classes to help students learn how to sew. This Makerspace combines art and math skills. Make a connection with a store that has fabric sample books. Ask them to donate those sample books to your Makerspaces, when they get new ones. Take the books apart and then organize the samples by color or design. They can be used for pillows, bracelets, purses, etc. The math skills come to the forefront when the students start to plan, cut, and put together their fabric in new ways.

If you have students who are involved in dance, they can utilize their skills in a Makerspace. You may not have space to dance in the library, but you have equipment that can be used by students. They can use a tablet or phone to store music. Practice their performance outside the library. Then use another device to take pictures or videos of their performance. Twenty-first-century technology has created an expectation of selfies for 21-st-century youngsters. Post them wherever your district gives approval.

Depending upon your tolerance for noise, you can put out commercially made musical instruments and let students explore with them. If you would like to add a keyboard, guitar, or small drum to your collection, take a look in the local second-hand store. Use a tablet to record the creative compositions. Once children are excited about music, they might want to create their own musical instrument. Add empty containers to make drums and bells, chenille sticks to make bell sticks, and toilet paper rolls, rice, and washi tape to make maracas. Of course, include books about music play in that Makerspace.

Most elementary students have experiences with crayons, but they may not have gotten to use a lot of other media. Examine your collection to see which of your books are illustrated with chalk or markers. Include them as a part of this art Makerspace. Chalk is relatively inexpensive, which makes it a good choice for Makerspaces. It can change appearances depending upon the paper it is used on. Include colored paper as well as white paper for students to use. Cut the paper in half and it will last longer. Children love to use markers and dry erase markers can provide hours of entertainment. If you go to one of the big box stores, they will cut a big sheet of white board into individual sheets that can be used in your Makerspace.

Children hear sound effects when they listen to movies, TV, or video games. Give them a chance to try and make their own sound effects and use them in their writing and video productions. Provide sound effects for them to hear. Give them directions for a few simple sound effects. Let them have a chance to experiment with a variety of materials to create their own sound effects. Students can take those skills and add them to their stories or videos.

Many children use colored pencils, but not very many have used watercolor colored pencils. They are so much less messy to use that they are a great choice for a Makerspace. Be sure the package clearly identifies them as watercolor colored pencils. When using them, color with the pencils as normal. Then use a small brush and add just a little water to the drawing. It gives a different look than either straight watercolor or colored pencil. Collage is a striking illustration style and it is one that students enjoy doing. You can set up the opportunity by providing a variety of papers and glue, and paper and pencils. The paper and pencils provide the tools to sketch a draft. The papers and glue allow Makers to create the actual collage.

For those schools that have music teachers, children get lots of opportunity to sing. However, for those students who don't have the opportunity to receive music instruction, we can offer them a chance to share their musical skills. Our collections can include books of songs and recordings that children can enjoy. Then we can create a Makerspace where youngsters can practice and share their talent. Provide some sound tracks for your Makers to use as background music. Talk to your music teacher about what tools he or she has available and would be willing to share with you.

The arts are so broad. They allow children the chance to express their individuality and develop some skills that could develop into adult hobbies. Unfortunately, they are sometimes eliminated from elementary schools. Makerspaces can provide an opportunity for children to enjoy those activities. For additional arts curriculum ideas, explore these websites.

**Kennedy Center ArtsEdge**—http://artsedge.kennedy-center.org/educators/standards.aspx
Standards are divided by K–4, 5–8, and 9–12 configurations. You can search by grade band and arts genre.

**National Association for Music Education**—http://www.nafme.org/my-classroom/standards/
There is a searchable link at this site to better access the 2014 Music Standards.

**National Art Education Association**—https://www.arteducators.org
Standards and lesson plans are included on this site.

**National Core Arts Standards**—http://www.nationalartsstandards.org
Standards for dance, media arts, music, theatre, and visual arts are included here.

# Ideas for Getting Started

## ARTS
### Bracelets

1. Get some ideas about jewelry creations by looking at the pictures in the books on the table. If you would like to see additional ideas, look in the 745 and 746 section of our library.

2. Create a pattern with the beads.

3. Tie a knot in the end of the string. String the beads. Tie a knot in the other end of the string.

4. Put the bracelet on and have a friend loosely tie the two ends together.

Create!

# Ideas for Getting Started

## ARTS
### Instruments

1. You will notice books on the table from the 745.5 and 784 sections of the library that give information about instruments.

2. Gently play the instruments that are here.

3. Enjoy the pictures of the handmade instruments.

4. Next, take some of the materials on the table and create your own musical instrument to take home.

5. Record music from one of the instruments.

# Ideas for Getting Started

## ARTS
## Origami

1. The pictures of finished origami from the 736 section books provide you a look of what you could create.

2. Choose a piece of paper to use and a pattern that you would like to follow.

3. Follow the directions the best you can. Remember it doesn't have to look exactly like the pictures.

4. When you get it finished, name it and take a photo of it. Post the picture on the Makerspace board.

Create!

# Ideas for Getting Started

## ARTS
## Performing a Play

1. There are some sample plays from the 812 section and Readers' Theater scripts on the table. Read one of them to get a sense of how they are written.

2. Write a script with a beginning, middle and end. Be sure you have included a plot, setting, and characters.

3. Practice your play with some of your friends.

4. Record your play and we'll post it.

Create!

# Ideas for Getting Started

## ARTS
## Fabric

1. You will find jewelry, pillow, and purse samples on the table, along with books from the 746 section. Think about the colors and patterns of the fabric and which ones you like.

2. Consider the fabric panels and what you want to make. Choose a piece of fabric that you like.

3. Pick up the directions sheet for your project. Follow the directions until you complete the project.

4. When your project is complete, take a picture of it and post it.

Create!

# Ideas for Getting Started

## ARTS
## Dance

1. Play some of your favorite music. View some of the books from the 792.8 section.

2. Create a one-minute dance to go along with it and practice it until you are comfortable performing it.

3. Write an introduction for your performance that includes the name of the music and the musical group.

4. Use the tripod or ask a friend to video your performance.

5. Post your video.

Create!

# Ideas for Getting Started

## ARTS
## Chalk/Dry Erase Markers

1.  Browse the books in this Makerspace. Some of them are from the 745.59 section, while others are illustrated with chalk or markers.

2.  Experiment with the chalk and dry erase markers.

3.  Create a picture that you are willing to let others see.

4.  Ask a friend to write a story, based on your illustration.

5.  Record the story and illustration.

Create!

# Ideas for Getting Started

## ARTS
## Sound Effects

1. Peruse the books from the 621.389 section about making sound effects.

2. Listen to sound effects from the recordings.

3. Create a few sound effects.

4. Add sound effects to one of your writing pieces or videos.

5. Share your project with others.

# Ideas for Getting Started

## ARTS
## Water Color Pencils and Collage

1. Thumb through the books on the table. Their illustrations are either watercolor or collage.

2. Take a piece of paper, a watercolor pencil, and a small paintbrush.

3. Color with the pencil. Get the brush barely wet and use it on the drawing.

4. Use several pieces of the colored paper and arrange it until you are satisfied with the arrangement. Glue the pieces down.

5. Share your work with others.

Create!

# Ideas for Getting Started

## ARTS
### Singing

1. Enjoy some of the books here or look for more in the 782.42 or 796.35 section of our library.

2. Listen to some of the music here.

3. Practice using one of the sound tracks and singing with it.

4. Record a final copy of your song.

5. Post it for others to enjoy.

# CHAPTER 8

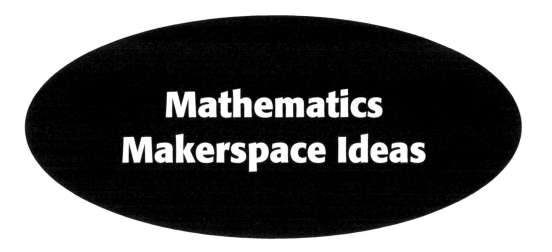

# Mathematics Makerspace Ideas

You may not think of math as being a viable topic for a Makerspace, but math offers many opportunities to create hands-on experiences.

Geometry provides the chance to utilize some materials that are probably in your school, but you've not used them in the library before. Ask around and you will likely find some math manipulatives that aren't being used. Put them into a Makerspace and students see them in a whole new light. Younger students match shapes. Older students label them with the proper names, make designs, or build with them.

Fractions are sometimes a difficult concept for youngsters to understand. If they get a chance to cut a whole into specific fractions, the concept becomes real. For an independently used Makerspace, put out samples of paper representing a variety of fractions and let them cut the different sizes. Children love cutting and get very little opportunity to practice that skill. If you want to focus on fractions during direct instruction, buy grapes, oranges, and apples. Using a child-friendly Halloween knife, have the children cut the grapes in half. Peel the orange and determine how many segments are in it. Talk about how each segment is a fraction of the orange. Cut the apple into a predetermined fraction. Children understand fractions better when they can see them. You can also tie this Makerspace to health standards.

Tangrams originated in China many years ago. People of all ages have enjoyed them ever since. Use Makerspaces to introduce these age-old math puzzles to a new generation. Put out sample puzzles and watch the students get excited. Have them create stories about their creation and you've included English language arts standards.

Young learners need to start with the basics when it comes to math, which means knowing the names of numbers and what they represent. Get a set of numbers or make a set of laminated paper ones. Put them in a container. Have children draw out a number, write the numeral for it, and draw the amount it represents. Post them on a number line in the media center.

Today's students often check the computer when they want to know the time. Since being able to tell time on a standard clock is a part of math standards, providing students with experiences to do that means an important standard and life skill can be a Makerspace. Start with a sample clock. Include smaller sample clocks for individual students to make with paper, paper fasteners, two paper clock hands, and a black marker. Students draw out a slip of paper that has time written on it. They draw that time on a sample clock with the marker. They choose another clock, clock hands, and paper fastener. They use those pieces to make a clock to take with them.

Teaching within a Makerspace can be a great experience for students and staff. Sequencing is a particular good math standard for direct instruction. Make a handout that shows dirt, containers, water, seeds, plant stalk, and blooming plant or print one from the Internet. Cut the segments apart ahead of time. Make them available for students to put in order. If possible, provide actual dirt, containers, water, and seeds, and lead the students through the planting process. The plants can be housed in the library or classroom for students to watch their growth. These actions not only support math standards, but also science standards about plant life cycle.

Another math standard students need to achieve is recognizing the different denominations of money. In an independent Makerspace, put the money out and let students use it in a multitude of ways. For example, they could show equal amounts of money, that is, four quarters equal one dollar equals ten dimes equal, etc. You can create money story problems and let students solve them. Another way to use the money and apply it to real life is to put out food, movie, or toy ads and have students figure out the cost for their family to purchase some of those items.

Dominoes can provide fun in a couple of different ways. First, they can be used to fulfill math standards. You can challenge youngsters to make patterns, do math processes with specific dominos, or play a standard domino game. If you want to place them in an engineering Makerspace, children can build with them. Dominoes provide a lot of bang for your buck.

One way to create open-ended materials for students is to give blank materials and then let them create their own specific product. For example, make blank puzzle pieces. Your school's production department may have a template to cut a variety of puzzle shapes. Lay them out and have students find two puzzles that match shape and add a math concept. Younger children create basic matches and older youngsters write more complex problems. You could also include art concepts by specifying the type of art used on the pieces.

Too often, students ask, "When will I ever use this?" as they learn a math concept. Help them see possible math careers with this Makerspace. Create a set of career cards. One side of the card says the name of the career. The other side gives a short explanation of what is involved in the career and the education that is needed to perform it. The students take a look at several cards and then choose one that seems interesting to them. Then they create a recording that includes the name of the career and what is included in the occupation. The recording plays on your news, or school library TV channel.

If you have math games available, encourage youngsters to play them. That will provide them with models that they can use to create their own math competitions. You could start a math game competition for your school.

Remember, Makerspaces come in many formats. Use your imagination as you create them for your students.

Mathematical websites to check out include:

**Awesome Library**—http://www.awesomelibrary.org/math.html
Standards and lesson plans are available on this site.

**Mathematical Association of America**—http://www.maa.org/programs/students/fun-math
This site includes various Math activities, some of which elementary students could enjoy.

**Math-Play.com**—http://www.math-play.com/Elementary-Math-Games.html
These Math games are listed by grade level, starting at first grade and going through fifth grade.

**National Council of Teachers of Mathematics**—http://www.nctm.org/standards/
The complete Principles and Standards for School Mathematics is a member-only resources, but the Executive Summary provides excellent information and is available for free on this site.

# Ideas for Getting Started

## MATH
### Tangrams

1. Tangrams started in China years ago and have been enjoyed by many people.

2. Take a look at the sample sheets.

3. Take the pieces and match them to the sample shapes.

4. Name what you have created. Write about it.

5. Draw a picture of your tangram and attach it to your story.

6. Additional tangram books can be found in the 703.73 section.

Create!

# Ideas for Getting Started

## MATH
### Fractions

1. Notice the fraction sample pictures on the table.

2. Looking at the samples, cut the shapes into fractions.

3. Label what you've cut with the correct fraction.

4. Either post your work on the bulletin board or record it and we'll post it.

5. You'll find books about fractions in the 510 section.

# Ideas for Getting Started

## MATH
### Dominoes

1. Try using the dominoes in different ways.

2. Make a pattern.

3. Choose any one domino. Draw a picture of it. Show math problems using the numbers on that domino.

4. Play dominoes by matching one end of a domino to another. Put double dominoes perpendicular to the rest of the dominoes.

# Ideas for Getting Started

## MATH
### Numbers

1. Choose a number from the container.

2. Using one of the papers on the table; write the numeral, and name for it.

3. Draw pictures that represent that number. Your drawings may be as detailed as you would like them to be. You may use markers or colored pencils.

4. Post your work on our number line.

# Ideas for Getting Started

## MATH
### Telling Time

1. Look at the large clock. Can you tell what time it shows?

2. Turn it over and read the time on the back of it. Were you right?

3. Take one of the small clocks and draw clock hands that show a specific time. Be sure to make one clock hand longer and one clock hand shorter.

4. Write the time on the back of the clock.

# Ideas for Getting Started

## MATH
### Sequence

1. Observe the blooming plant.

2. Look at the papers showing the steps in plant life cycle.

3. Put the steps in order and attach them to the Plant Life Cycle frame.

4. Collaborating with others, get a container, dirt, seeds, and water.

5. Put them together in proper sequence.

Create!

# Ideas for Getting Started

## MATH
## Money

1. Look at this play money and identify each piece.

2. Make at least two stacks of different denominations that equal each other.

3. Look at the ads. Find one item that you would like to own. Show how much money it would take to buy it.

4. Choose one of the story problem cards and figure out the money answer for each problem.

Create!

# Ideas for Getting Started

## MATH
### Math Puzzles

1. Choose two pieces that fit together.

2. On one of them write an equation. On the other piece, fill in the answer.

3. Consider adding appropriate artwork on the pieces. It could be artwork representing the math or it could be decorative art.

4. Add your puzzle pieces to the Math Puzzle Box.

# Ideas for Getting Started

## MATH
### Math Careers

1. From the Career Cards, choose one that appeals to you.

2. Practice saying the name of the occupation and what appeals to you about it.

3. When you are comfortable, video yourself. Start with your name. Next, say the name of the career. Last, explain what happens in the job, what type of education is needed and why the job appeals to you.

# CHAPTER 9

Social studies takes on a new appearance when you use that content in Makerspaces. If that seems impossible to you, then take took a closer look at your curriculum guides. Let your imagination go and come up with some options that work for your students. Here are some ideas to get you started.

The National Council for Social Studies (NCSS) themes include:

V. Individuals, Groups & Institutions Social studies programs should include experiences that provide for the study of interactions among individuals, groups and institutions.

Use that theme as a basis to create a heroes Makerspace. Use your biography section as the basis for this Makerspace. Students will choose a person that they think has done something really important and read about him or her. They will then write a script for a 30- to 60-second video that tells about their "hero." Post it wherever you have as an option.

As a part of social studies, children learn about the three branches of government. Makerspaces can provide the opportunity for them to imagine themselves being a part of government. Youngsters choose a branch that intrigues them. They project themselves as an adult government figure. Using a template you provide, they will be the Time Person of the Year and write a magazine article that focuses on how they have made a difference in people's lives by serving in that government position.

Certainly a part of social studies is learning how the world has changed over time. One aspect that clearly shows advancement is transportation. To engage youngsters in that concept, collect books about transportation and display them along with a challenge to create a 21st-century mode of transportation that hadn't been invented yet. Children's imaginative drawings are a pleasure to view. Their conversations about their creations are equally interesting. Students can create a newspaper or newspaper advertisement that includes their drawing and why someone would buy their imaginary invention.

At one time, the Pony Express was considered an amazingly fast way to communicate with others. Since then, we've had other ground-breaking communication inventions such as the

telegraph, telephone, and the Internet. Today's generation of students could be the inventors of the next generation of communication tools. The National Council of Social Studies VI. Science, Technology, & Society states "Social Studies programs should include experiences that provide for the study of relationships among science, technology and society" (NCSS, n.d.). This Makerspace could encourage young inventors to reach new heights. Make books available that focus on communication tools. Ask students to make a communication timeline that includes two tools that have been invented and the last one being their invention. Draw and write about their invention. Write and make a video that is a 20- to 30-second commercial about their invention.

One segment of social studies is geography. Our world seems smaller with today's technology giving access to people from everywhere. However, that doesn't mean children actually know the location of countries or how to read a map. Today's students think of maps as something you see on a phone. This independent Makerspace includes books about maps, paper, maps, and pencils. Students could draw a map of their neighborhood, or label one of the school campus or the school library. You could also make a state or national map. As a direct instruction Makerspace activity with a whole class, make salt and flour maps showing the areas that Native Americans historically inhabited, based on your social studies text.

The Library of Congress website provides a wealth of information. Introduce students to it and you've unlocked a treasure trove of material for them. This Makerspace is a great way to help youngsters understand primary and secondary sources. Define the difference between the two types of sources. Bring the Library of Congress site up on a device. Children choose a topic of interest and find a primary source about the topic. They read it and then write a secondary source about it.

As students study economics in social studies, they need to learn the difference between goods, services, wants, and needs. One way to learn those concepts is through a Makerspace experience. First, students need to understand the definitions for the four terms. You can put out books that explain the terms or define them in the "Ideas for Getting Started" sheets. The students draw and label a picture of a good or service and one picture of a want or need. The students then make a paper slide video that is created by videoing and narrating the drawings.

Another social studies area of study is citizenship. Helping youth to understand the value of developing good civic virtues will make the world better for everyone. Provide books that focus on characteristics of good citizens. The instruction can start early by explaining why school procedures should be followed. Have the students do a quick role-playing of good behavior at school or at home.

An important aspect of social studies is learning about cultures. Help students to learn about a specific culture that interests them. For students who know their family heritage or culture, let them focus on one of them. Some children may not know that information, so they can choose any culture that interests them. They can share their family customs and investigate how others from that area celebrate holidays or if there are particular foods that are special.

Understanding other time periods sometimes stretches the imaginations of youngsters. We can help them make the leap from the world they live in to previous time periods through a variety of experiences. Start with a Makerspace that includes information about previous time periods. You could pull books or you could make fact sheets. Once students have those facts, they can decide which fact is most interesting to them, make a representation of it, and share with others.

Social studies is a wide field of information. It will provide lots of opportunities for Makerspace experiences. For additional social studies information, go to the following sites.

**USA.gov**—https://www.usa.gov/teachers
This site replaced the kids.gov site. It now offers lesson plans for teachers.

**National Council for Geographic Education**—http://www.ncge.org
The K–12 Teacher Resources provide loads of ideas for anyone interested in exciting students about geography.

**National Council for the Social Studies**—http://www.socialstudies.org
This site includes the social studies standards as well as the annual bibliography of Notable Social Studies Trade Books for Young People.

**Teacher Vision**—https://www.teachervision.com/games/social-studies/48746.html
Games and puzzles for the K–5 crowd are the highlight of this page.

## Reference

National Council for the Social Studies. "National Curriculum Standards for Social Studies: Chapter 2—The Themes of Social Studies." https://www.socialstudies.org/standards/strands

# Ideas for Getting Started

## SOCIAL STUDIES
### Heroes

1. Choose one of the books from the table or visit the biography section to choose one about a person that interests you.

2. Read the book and look to find out what that person did that was important.

3. Create a 30- to 60-seconds video about the person and his or her accomplishments.

4. It will be posted on the media center TV.

# Ideas for Getting Started

## SOCIAL STUDIES
### Branches of Government

1. Take a look at the books on the table and the poster showing the three branches of government.

2. Consider which one of the branches looks most interesting to you.

3. Using the Time Person of the Year template, take a selfie and put it in the template.

4. Write about how you help others through that job.

# Ideas for Getting Started

## SOCIAL STUDIES
## Transportation

1. From the books on the table, notice the changes over time in transportation.

2. Imagine a yet-to-be designed type of transportation.

3. Draw what it will look like and how it will move.

4. Create a print advertisement for it.

5. Post it in the Makerspace Notebook.

# Ideas for Getting Started

## SOCIAL STUDIES
## Communication

1. Take a look at these books from the 302.2 section.

2. Use the timeline template and put in any two tools that have already been invented.

3. Create a new communication tool for the third one.

4. Draw and write about your new invention.

5. Write and make a video that is a 20- to 30-second commercial about your invention.

Create!

# Ideas for Getting Started

## SOCIAL STUDIES
### Geography

1. Look at the books on the table showing maps of different geographic areas.

2. Think about an area that you know well enough to draw a map of the area.

3. Draw the perimeter, label the directions and name the area.

4. Fill in at least four important details to that area.

5. Post in the Makerspace Notebook.

Create!

# Ideas for Getting Started

## SOCIAL STUDIES
## Primary and Secondary Sources

1. A primary source is from someone who was at the event. A secondary source comes from someone who was not at the event.

2. Go to this Library of Congress Primary Source Set website: http://www.loc.gov/teachers/classroommaterials/primarysourcesets/?loclr=blogtea

3. Choose a topic that interests you. Read one of the primary sources.

4. Write a secondary source account.

Create!

# Ideas for Getting Started

## SOCIAL STUDIES
## Economic Terms

1. A good is something that you can pay for and physically touch. A service is something you pay for and is done for you. Wants are something you would like to have. Needs are something you must have to live.
2. Draw a picture of a service or good and label it.
3. Draw a picture of a want or need and label it.
4. Make a paper slide video with your drawings.

Create!

# Ideas for Getting Started

## SOCIAL STUDIES
### Citizenship

1. Take a look at the books on the table. They are from the 300s section of the library.

2. In one of the books find an example of making a good choice at home.

3. In one of the books find an example of making a good choice at school.

4. Create and video a short play of a child choosing to make a good citizen choice.

5. Load the video to play on the library TV.

# Ideas for Getting Started

## SOCIAL STUDIES
### Cultures

1. Take a look at the globe and locate some countries that interest you.

2. Talk to your family and see if they know of other countries that are a part of your family's history.

3. Investigate a country that your family has connections to or that you have a special interest in.

4. On a poster, name the country, give 3 pieces of information about it and say what interests you about it.

# Ideas for Getting Started

## SOCIAL STUDIES
### History

1. Take a look at the information on the table.

2. Choose a time period that interests you.

3. Look for facts about their clothing, home, or foods.

4. Choose one thing to make that represents that time period to you. It could be a hat, a representation of the housing or a recipe that was current in that time.

# CHAPTER 10

## Language Arts Makerspace Ideas

Language arts curriculum includes reading, writing, speaking, listening, viewing, and visual representation. It is the content most often thought of in connection with traditional school libraries. You can make great Makerspaces with these language arts concepts.

Writing has been a point of emphasis in educational testing for several years now. Makerspaces can bring the fun back to writing. Start by connecting to the current excitement about super heroes. Set out super hero books. Encourage children to create their own super hero by writing and drawing about a person or animal that has special characteristics. Place their finished product in the Makerspace Writers Notebook. Of course, you can also use story starters or ask students to create a new ending to one of their favorite stories. Make writing more personal with students writing about their favorite activities. A bulletin board where they can post pictures of themselves participating in a favorite activity and their writing about it quickly becomes a high interest space in the library.

Connect language arts to social studies. Many fifth-grade classrooms study the United States during social studies. Challenge youngsters to create a public relations brochure for a state.

They will need to do some basic fact-finding. They will use your print collection to learn facts. Then they will take that information and turn it into persuasive writing to encourage tourists to visit their chosen state. This technique could be used for fourth graders who generally study their own state or for countries, if students are learning about other countries. Tourist brochures can be displayed in the library.

Speaking allows for lots of student opportunities to share their thoughts. Today's technology provides formats that previous generations of youngsters wouldn't have had available. Our students found paper slides to be a great way to share their ideas. They draw their ideas and then provide a narrative for the pictures, as they are videoed. It is a technique that works for a variety of ages and content areas. Some of our students created them as book summaries while others showed processes they were studying.

Reading aloud sessions are a part of traditional school library experiences, but they can expand into Makerspaces. After the read-aloud chapter, each student makes notes about the main idea and three details that they remember. They talk about their ideas in pairs and then the whole group agrees on a set of information. After that, they work in small groups to put their notes together, draw one set of pictures, and create a narrative for it. Video their work and you have a complete retelling of the story. The experience includes so many of the language arts skills and it blends traditional direct instruction and library activities with 21st-century Makerspaces.

Viewing and visual representation can blend with an art Makerspace. If you display the works of illustrators and provide materials for children to create artwork based on the illustrators' techniques, you've created a multicurricular Makerspace. To do that, you can put out art materials that are labeled with the illustrators' names. Children can match a specific illustrator's name to the art materials. Recognizing illustrators' styles helps youngsters to be differentiating readers as they enjoy picture books.

Another way to connect language arts and arts standards is to create graphic novels. This often makes a good collaborative project. Students love reading the format, so creating it draws them into the reading and writing process. Students peruse the books and then create their own graphic novel. When they are finished, publish a copy and keep it on display in the library.

Each state has a recommended book list. Let your students help promote those books. Give them a choice of creating a print ad or a video commercial. There is nothing like a peer review to send books flying off the shelf. Youngsters love others seeing their work.

Offer to make equipment available during students' recess time. Their creativity will flow as they have the freedom to work independently. Encourage them to create their own videos. They can write plays, tape library procedures, or make a content video such as science processes. The experiences help them to be more comfortable speaking in front of groups. Buy "green suits," which will allow them to utilize some special effects.

There are two sides to any issue. Let students practice their persuasive writing by setting up debates. Topics could be driven by students' interests. For example: should we wear uniforms, should there be more recess time, or should lunchtime be longer? The debates can also be on a social studies topic such as who is the most important 20th-century U.S. president or a science idea like which 20th-century invention changed the world the most.

Students need to know how to compare and contrast. Help them practice that concept by setting up this Makerspace. Combine pairs of books that tell the same story. Students need to read both books. Then they create a Venn diagram that compares and contrasts the two texts. Display their work along with the books on a library counter.

Regardless of what students do as adults, they will need to use language arts skills. These Makerspaces provide them a chance to practice those abilities. Language arts websites abound. Use these to get additional ideas.

**International Literacy Association**—https://www.literacyworldwide.org/get-resources
Annual Children's Choices Reading Lists are archived on this site.

**National Association for the Education of Young Children**—http://www.naeyc.org/files/naeyc/file/positions/PSREAD98.PDF
A position statement about reading and writing from IRA and NAEYC.

**National Council of Teachers of English**—http://www.ncte.org
This site contains a wealth of information, including NCTE/IRA standards.

**ReadWriteThink**—http://www.readwritethink.org/about/our-partners/international-reading-association-1.html
This site is supported by the International Literacy Association (formerly the International Reading Association) and National Council of Teachers of English. There are several classroom resources that could be tweaked and used for Makerspaces.

**Reading Rockets**—http://www.readingrockets.org/article/25-activities-reading-and-writing-fun
The U.S. Department of Education publishes a list of 25 activities for Reading and Writing Fun on this site.

# Ideas for Getting Started

## LANGUAGE ARTS
### Super Heroes—Super Powers

1. Take a look at these Super Hero books from the 398.2 and 741.5 sections of our library.

2. Imagine a person or animal with special powers.

3. Write a story about your newly invented character.

4. Draw illustrations to go along with it.

5. Put your finished product in the Makerspace Writers Notebook.

# Ideas for Getting Started

## LANGUAGE ARTS
### Special Places

1. Choose a state or country that you are interested in.

2. Search in the 900s for a book about that area.

3. Create a brochure that encourages visitors to visit the place.

4. Include pictures and text.

5. Display your brochure with the United States or world map.

# Ideas for Getting Started

## LANGUAGE ARTS
### Paper Slides

1. Choose one of the books you just finished reading.

2. Create at least three paper slides about the book. They need to include a cover slide, one that shows characters, setting, and plot and one that shows why you liked the book.

3. Video the paper slides, while you narrate them.

4. Post your finished product on the library TV channel.

Create!

# Ideas for Getting Started

## LANGUAGE ARTS
### Video Production

1. Think about what type of video you would like to make: personally written play, capture subject content, etc.

2. Write the script and practice it.

3. Explore using the "green suits."

4. Complete your production.

5. Post your video on the library TV channel.

# Ideas for Getting Started

## LANGUAGE ARTS
### Read Aloud

1. Listen to the read aloud.

2. When the chapter is finished, write what you think is the main idea and three details. Share your ideas with a buddy.

3. Collaborate with a small group to create paper slides about this story.

4. Narrate the paper slides while you video them.

5. Post the video.

# Ideas for Getting Started

## LANGUAGE ARTS
### Illustration Styles

1. Choose one of the illustrators represented by the books on the table.

2. Write the illustrator's name in the center of a card. Write adjectives that describe the illustrators' work.

3. Match your chosen illustrator's name to the art materials that also have illustrators' names.

4. Create the illustrator's style as best you can.

# Ideas for Getting Started

## LANGUAGE ARTS
## Graphic Novels

1. Look at the graphic novels from the 741.5 section of the library.

2. Notice how the author and illustrator have blended words and pictures.

3. Create a new character.  Set a location. Provide a plot for the character.  Add some additional characters.

4. Draft, revise, and edit your work.

5. Publish your work within one of our book covers.

Create!

# Ideas for Getting Started

## LANGUAGE ARTS
### State Book Lists Promotion

1. Choose your favorite book that you read from the state book lists.

2. Make a print ad that will encourage someone else to read one of the books.

3. If you prefer, create a video commercial to excite someone to read the book you like.

4. Either post your print ad on the state book list display or post the video on the library TV channel.

Create!

# Ideas for Getting Started

## LANGUAGE ARTS
### Debates

1. Choose a topic with two sides.

2. Find a friend who will take the other side of the topic.

3. Each of you write reasons why your side is "right."

4. Record each of your "persuasive" ideas.

5. Ask a small group to vote on one side or the other of the issue.

# Ideas for Getting Started

## LANGUAGE ARTS
## Compare and Contrast

1. Choose a pair of books that tell the same story.

2. Draw a Venn diagram.

3. In the outside of one circle, write the title of one book and details about that version.

4. In the outside of the other circle, write the title of the other book and details about it.

5. In the center, where the circle overlapped, write what occurs in both books.

Create!

# CHAPTER 11

# Health Makerspace Ideas

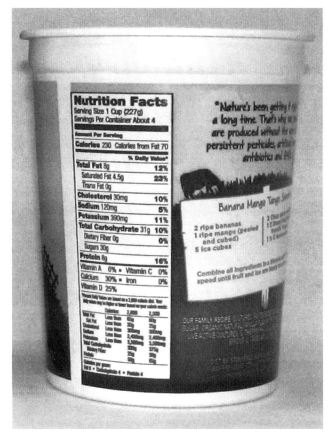

Health is not a tested curriculum, so it may not get taught as consistently as reading or math. The content might be rolled into the physical education or science curriculum. Regardless of where your district makes the connection, it is important for our children to know how to make healthy choices. A Makerspace can provide that opportunity for them.

To help youngsters better understand nutrition, set up empty containers of food and make a guessing game as to which has the most sugar, calories, fat, etc. Then ask them to plan a healthy snack from the ingredients. Another option could include putting out the grocery ads from the newspaper, paper plates, and have them cut out from the newspaper and paste on the plate the nutrient-rich food that they would eat. You can also set up empty containers and have students create healthy meal menus from them. It gives them a whole new look at breakfast, lunch, dinner, and snacks. Recent research shows that obesity abounds in our society today. Let's help children learn to think about what they put in their bodies, not just mindlessly consume food.

Children don't always see the if/then consequences of their actions. We can help them be more aware. One way to develop awareness is to have them make safety posters. For example, if you run into someone, you are both more likely to be hurt, than if you are walking. Since the final product will be a poster, you could include art standards, too. Their work will be posted around campus.

Bullying seems to be an issue in our culture today. We want to help our students be model citizens and display good mental health choices. Let them know there are books that deal with the issue. Share a storyboard form with them. Choose an audience for the video. They need to decide are they speaking to the bully, the bullied, or an observer? Have them plan out their video on the form. Use the storyboard as a basis to video the storyboard.

Getting a good night's sleep is important for all of us. Youngsters tend to be so busy now with lots of activities and screens, that they don't always realize how tired they have become. The Centers for Disease Control and Prevention says children ages six to twelve should get nine to twelve hours of sleep every day. Put out books about sleep. Provide a sleep chart for students and ask them to fill it in for a week. It provides a very personal look at their sleep habits. This is a good activity for parent Makerspace events, because they play such a powerful part in children's bedtime habits, but youngsters can do their own tracking.

Learning to manage your emotions sometimes takes a lifetime. Help children get started by trying this Makerspace. Share books that represent various emotions. Ask children to

choose two emotions to draw and write about healthy ways to express them. Let them video representations of the feelings. If we can help young ones learn to express emotions in appropriate ways, everyone benefits.

A part of good health is exercising regularly. Challenge students to make a one-week calendar of exercising that includes three different exercises they would find fun to do. Talk with your physical education teachers to see how they might have input into this activity. The students can record a demo of how to do a specific exercise.

A part of health can be taking care of the world by reducing, reusing, and recycling. This Makerspace shows youth that recycling can be fun. Parents willingly donate toilet paper and paper towel tubes, if they know you want them. Place the tubes and tape on the table. Add some markers to the materials for students to use so they can decorate and then name their marble run.

If you're thinking about health, you have to think about the body. Provide a picture of the body that shows the basic organs and where they are located. Get some butcher paper, scissors, pencils, and markers. Have the students work in pairs or triads. One child will lie down on the paper and another person will draw around them. Each child will draw in basic organs on their body outline.

According to the Illinois Department of Public Health (http://www.idph.state.il.us/public/hb/hbsmoke.htm), the average age of a new smoker is thirteen. Children need to see reasons for not smoking before they reach that age. Your Health Makerspace could have paper, markers, etc. for students to make posters in support of a world that has tobacco-free kids.

Health is a very personal subject. There are some basic facts that are true for everyone, but after that people make individual decisions or just fall into habits without really thinking about what they are doing. We want children to make a conscious decision about their health goals. This Makerspace can help children know there are decisions to be made. Create a checklist for the children to fill out about their health habits. The product is theirs to keep, rather than to share.

Depending upon your physical space and local codes, you could make some healthy snacks, too. At one of your parent nights, make ice cream with frozen bananas. Add fruit to the bananas to create a variety of flavors. Since the parents are there, you can be sure that no food allergy will go unnoticed. The experience also includes some math concepts, since you cut and measure the ingredients.

If your school uses the D.A.R.E. program, talk to the officer in charge and see how you could collaborate to support the anti-drug message. Making videos could be a good choice to help students remember the content.

While health isn't a part of state testing, children need to learn good health habits. Makerspaces can be one tool to help that happen. Find out who teaches health in your school and talk to them about other possible Makerspace activities. Use these websites for current information.

**Centers for Disease Control and Prevention**—http://www.cdc.gov/healthyschools/sher/standards/index.htm
National standards and indicators are listed here.

**Drug Abuse Resistance Education**—http://www.dare.org
If your school participates in the D.A.R.E. program, this site could be helpful to you.

**Nutrition.gov**—http://www.nutrition.gov/life-stages/children
This site provides information and activities to help youngsters make better food choices.

**Society of Health and Physical Educators**—http://www.shapeamerica.org/standards/health/
2007 National Health Education Standards are given here.

## Resource

Illinois Department of Public Health. "Smoking." Health Beat. http://www.idph.state.il.us/public/hb/hbsmoke.htm

# Ideas for Getting Started

## HEALTH
### Nutrition

1. Look at the food containers and notice the numbers for sugar, fat, salt, and calories. Study the "Choose My Plate" picture.

2. Using that information, plan a healthy snack that you would eat.

3. Next, take a paper plate and fill it with pictures of nutritious food that you like for breakfast, lunch, or dinner.

4. Make a video telling about your choices and why you made them.

Create!

# Ideas for Getting Started

## HEALTH
### Safety

1. Take a look at the books on the table that came from the 363 section of the library.

2. Think about places where safety reminders could prevent accidents: for example, walking in the halls or putting away toys so no one trips on them.

3. Choose one of the papers from the table, make a draft, and then the final poster.

Create!

# Ideas for Getting Started

## HEALTH
### Bullying

1.  Scan the books on the table.  They are from the 300 section of the library.

2.  Draw a storyboard that shows a bullying situation getting resolved.

3.  Recruit friends to be in your movie.

4.  Video your friends performing your storyboard.

5.  Post it to be played on the media center TV.

Create!

# Ideas for Getting Started

## HEALTH
## Sleep

1. Browse the books about sleep.

2. Pick up the sleep chart on the table. For the next week, track what you do for an hour before bedtime, what time you go to bed, when you get up, and how you feel when you wake up.

3. Do you see a connection between how much sleep you get and how you feel?

4. Make a plan for you to get enough sleep.

Create!

# Ideas for Getting Started

## HEALTH
### Emotions

1. Look at the books on the table from the 152.4 section.

2. Choose two emotions and draw a face that represents each one.

3. Think about what is a healthy way to express those emotions.

4. Create a video that shows at least two emotions.

5. Post it to play on the library TV.

# Ideas for Getting Started

## HEALTH
## Exercise

1. Look at one of the exercise videos on the computer.

2. Track your exercise for a week. How long do you walk each day? Do you swim? Do you play a sport? Do you dance?

3. Think about an exercise that you enjoy that you could perform for a video.

4. Make a video that shows you performing the exercise and narrating it.

# Ideas for Getting Started

## HEALTH
### Reduce, Reuse, Recycle

1. Enjoy the books from the 363.72 section.

2. Reuse and recycle paper towel and toilet paper roll tubes by putting them together with tape to make a marble run.

3. Decorate and name it when you finish.

4. Take a video of you using the marble run.

# Ideas for Getting Started

## HEALTH
## Human Body

1. Look at the picture of the body with the organs identified.

2. Collaborate with a friend or two on this project.

3. Each person will draw around another person, so that each has his or her body outline.

4. Draw the organs in the body and label them.

5. Post on the Makerspace bulletin board.

# Ideas for Getting Started

## HEALTH
### Smoking Prevention

1. Browse the books from the 616.86 section.

2. Consider what will help people consider not smoking.

3. Draft, revise, and edit a poster.

4. Finalize your poster using the paper, pencils, and markers.

5. Place it on the Makerspace bulletin board.

Create!

# Ideas for Getting Started

## HEALTH
## Personal Health Goals

1. Pick up a Personal Health Goal Sheet.

2. Check off the number of foods you eat, the hours you sleep, and the time you exercise.

3. Make a plan that will help you to be healthy.

4. Track your behavior for a week.

# CHAPTER 12

## Data Collection, Assessment, and Evaluation in a Makerspace

Today's educational climate demands data collection. As school librarians, we are used to tracking circulations data and assessing our instruction. We can provide data, but we need to think about the big picture, as well as the details. Start by putting it into the familiar big picture in terms of: who, what when, where, why, and how.

## Data Collection

*Who* will see it? Within those groups, are there sub groups to consider? Think about specific grade levels and their involvement.

Students?

Teachers?

Administration?

Parents?

Community?

*What* do they want to know? Different audiences often want different information.

What are the materials that are being used?

What are the number of students who use it?

What do the students do there?

*When* will you gather the data and share it? Students and teachers could sign in as they use the Makerspaces. If you already do monthly or annual reports, then this data can be added to them. If not, consider what means you already have in place to share information and then add this data to it.

Daily?

Weekly?

Monthly?

Annually?

*Where* will important places be for Makerspaces? Think about location of the actual Makerspaces, but you also have to plan for storage of the materials. Where will you keep track of what materials you have?

Where are the Makerspaces located?

Where will the data collection take place?

Where will you store materials?

Where will you go for financial support?

*Why* do you track data? Collecting data takes time, so you need to have a clear reason as to why you are choosing to do it.

Why would someone give money or materials to a program, if they have no information about it?

Why would you have a program that you can't prove positively impacts students?

*How* you will gather the data? When possible, make the data collection as stress free as possible. It shouldn't be too time consuming for either you or the students. For example, consider having sign in sheets in the Makerspace Lab. They can tell who participated and which stations they used. It is information that can be used to show that the material benefits students and may help to gain possible additional acquisitions.

You also have to think about how the Makerspace was used. Was it a part of direct instruction? If so, then you may be able to use more traditional types of assessment, such as evaluation of the product and a rubric of the experience. If the Makerspace time was an exploration time, then a survey showing the students' reactions could give pertinent data.

Will the students sign in/check off their name when they use a Makerspace?

Will students track which Makerspace they use?

Will you use surveys? Exit cards?

What data will we collect and with whom will we share it?

What formative assessments would be helpful?

When do you want to do summative assessments?

If you feel like that is a lot of questions to think about, you are right. However, asking them early on will make your data collection more efficient and give you the data that you really are interested in having; it follows the old saying of "measure once and cut twice." Think carefully about what you want to know and why before you begin and then plan accordingly.

# Assessment and Evaluation

When you were getting your college degrees, you probably took a class that dealt with statistics, evaluation, and assessment. While the basic concepts remain, I recently read several articles to try and be able to give clear definitions of assessment, evaluation, and data collection. I've provided definitions, as I understand the terms. Feel free to utilize the terms as is most applicable in your school.

Formative assessment measures the experience while it is happening. That can be something that the youngster gives input for, as well as observations by others. You do that automatically as children work and you redirect them or give them additional information to help them be successful.

Questions to be considered could be:

Is the child enjoying the experience?

Is he staying on task?

What is he accomplishing?

Summative assessment measures knowledge and skills at the end of the experience. Grades are one example of summative assessment. There can be a self-assessment, something that someone else assesses, or a combination of the two. You may have a rubric or checklist of what was to be accomplished during the time.

For example you could ask one of the following:

What did the child learn by the end of the activity?

What did he produce as a final product?

What did the participant think of the activity?

Some of the experiences in the Makerspaces may indeed have a summative or evaluation attached to them. Particularly when you are using it for direct instruction. However, there won't always need to be a summative component. For example, if students are participating in an after-school event, you may or may not want a formal assessment of it. If you're asking for one, know what you are going to do with it.

According to the Institute for Teaching, Learning and Academic Leadership (http://www.itlal.org/?q=node/93), "evaluation is the process of observing and measuring a thing for the purpose of judging it and of determining its "value," either by comparison to similar things, or to a standard".

# Helpful Data Collection Websites

**American Society for Quality**—http://asq.org/learn-about-quality/data-collection-analysis-tools/overview/overview.html
This site shows various tools that could be used for data collection.

**Helpful Assessment Websites**—Some come from a school library viewpoint, while others show a Makerspace point of view.

**Educscapes**—http://eduscapes.com/sms/program/evaluation.html
An evaluation for the entire library program.

**Eductopia**—http://www.edutopia.org/blog/creating-authentic-maker-education-rubric-lisa-yokana
One person's ideas on how to create a Makerspace rubric.

**Ict4kids.ca**—https://ict4kids.ca/2016/04/04/what-does-assessment-look-like-in-makerspaces/
What does assessment look like in Makerspaces?

**A Planning Guide for Empowering Learners**—http://www.ala.org/aasl/standards/planning
This source looks at the entire library program.

**Research Related to School Libraries**—http://www.cde.ca.gov/ci/cr/lb/research.asp
A variety of research about school libraries

**Worlds of Learning**—http://worlds-of-learning.com/2016/05/31/flipping-assessment-in-a-makerspace-on-its-head/
Traditional assessment may not be the best tool for a Makerspace

Data collection, assessment, and evaluation are important tools to use because they show the people who donated products or money that they made a difference for students. They benefit students and teachers because they can show progress. They are important to us as Makerspace creators, since that information can help us know how the space and materials are used and give us information to improve them.

## Reference

Institute for Teaching, Learning and Academic Leadership. (n.d.) "What Is the difference between 'Assessment' and 'Evaluation'?" http://www.itlal.org/?q=node/93

# CHAPTER 13

**Funding a Makerspace**

Most activities in life require some amount of money and Makerspaces will need funding, too. Since they have become so popular, some companies offer kits of materials. If you have the funds to buy them, that can be great. However, don't feel like you have to choose from pre-packaged kits. You can easily start them with materials that are already at your school. Since most library budgets are already stretched to capacity, we will look at additional funding sources. Common possibilities are PTO/A funds, grants, district science dollars, donations, book fairs, flea markets, and yard sales.

Start with your local PTO/A. If you haven't already built a relationship with them, now is the perfect time to do it. They can be great advocates for you, if they understand what you are doing. Start with explaining Makerspaces and why they are important for students. Show how you've used some of the materials already available in the school. When you ask for dollars, specify equipment that you need to meet a particular curriculum standard. This organization is focused on your students and staff, so they make the perfect financial supporter for Makerspaces.

Then check for available money from local, state, and national grants. See if there is someone in your school district who writes grants. If so, they could be a great source in finding appropriate grants for you. If there is no district grant writer, look first in your community. Is there an educational foundation that funds teachers' projects? Visit local businesses. Some of them offer grants to educators. Check out your state's education department website and see what opportunities they provide. Many of the federal grants are distributed to the states and then individual programs are awarded grants from the state.

Nationally, there are several options available. As you look for grants, be aware of deadline dates. Some stay open continually for submission, which is called a rolling deadline and others have firm date deadlines. Depending upon what you are trying to fund, you might investigate one of the following sites:

**National Science Foundation**—http://www.nsf.gov/funding/education.jsp?fund_type=4
This section of the site is aimed at the K–12 audiences, but there is another section that lists more grants in alphabetical order.

**Honda Power of Dreams**—http://www.honda.com/community
If you have a Honda plant close to you, check out this community section to see how they have previously supported communities. Your Makerspace might be next.

**Toshiba Teacher Grants**
K–5 http://toshiba.com/taf/k5.jsp
6–12 http://toshiba.com/taf/612.jsp
Since elementary schools sometimes include grade 6, both Toshiba sites are included. The site says grants are open to teachers and are due by October first or the first business day after October 1 each year.

**Lockheed Martin STEM Grants**—http://expandedschools.org/funding-opportunities/
lockheed-martin-stem-grants#sthash.SHTdknp1.YyMSKFQj.dpbs
As the name makes clear, this site is focused on STEM opportunities.

A little research will provide additional grant opportunities. While that does involve some time, we are research specialists. We will just be using those skills to provide funding this time, instead of assisting students with projects.

Your district may distribute dollars for science instruction. This could be the perfect time to ask for a piece of that pie. Make the connection to your district science standards with the Makerspace that you want to create. Show how the experience will impact student achievement.

Look for donations. Never underestimate the power of the word, "please." Utilize your school's website or newspaper to tell about your Makerspaces and ask for donations. You can use empty paper towel rolls and toilet paper tubes to make a multitude of items. Along with tape, they can be turned into a marble run that demonstrates gravity or make a speaker system for a cell phone. Families like feeling that they are a part of the process and it also shows that recycling can be fun.

Another donation source could be your local high school. Many of those students have outgrown building materials that elementary students love. Contacting the local Honor Society or student government faculty representative could provide a lot of materials that are expensive in a store, but the donation makes a great community service project for high school students.

Consider some of the online organizations that support teacher needs. You never know when someone will look at your request and choose to fund it. There are no application fees, so it is worth a try. If you have a volunteer who writes well and has available time, applying for grants could be the perfect way for he or she to support the library program. Check with your building administrator to see if the school district has any parameters in place about applying for grants.

**Donors Choose**—https://www.donorschoose.org
This site was started by a teacher to help other teachers. You have to create a sign in, but there is no fee.

**Edutopia**—http://www.edutopia.org/grants-and-resources
Look at the long list of grants that are available. Just be sure that what you are asking matches the grant perimeters.

**Fund for Teachers**—http://www.fundforteachers.org
You can apply for personal and professional growth experiences that will impact your teaching.

**GetEdFunding**—http://www.getedfunding.com/c/index.web?s@uk4wLlOD6dR.Y
This site hosts educational funding opportunities for a variety of sources.

**Teach**—https://teach.com/what/grants-for-teachers/
This site breaks the grants listed into four broad categories, which can save time if you are only interested in applying for certain kinds.

**Teachers Count**—http://www.teacherscount.org/grants/
You will find a list of grants there. There are also contests available.

If you host book fairs, that can be another source of funding. There may be items available from the book fair source that can be used in Makerspaces. Hopefully, you also make some profit from the event and that could be used for some starter materials.

Shop at yard sales and flea markets. Sometimes you hear someone say, "Teachers work 8 to 3." We know better. We are educators 24/7. So when you are shopping at a flea market or yard sale, keep your eyes open for Makerspace possibilities. You want to choose items that can be cleaned and disinfected before you take them to school. You will be amazed at the quantity and quality of materials available from these sources.

It would be great if your school had a money tree and you just picked the amount of money you wanted and bought whatever you thought your students needed. However, that is never going to happen, so plan accordingly. You don't have to have thousands of dollars to start Makerspaces. You do need some creativity, a willingness to see materials in a new light, and a few dollars to get started. These ideas will help you get the small amount of money you need initially.

# CHAPTER 14

# Public Relations for a Makerspace

Once you are committed to creating Makerspaces and have funded them, you want to be sure others know about them. This is no time to hide your light under a bushel. By nature, educators don't tend to be people who brag about their accomplishments. You need to share about your Makerspaces so others know the great things that are being done for students in the library media center.

Your staff will be the first group to learn about this addition to the school library. You can announce it in a staff meeting, but they will remember it more clearly if they get to use the materials. You could have a staff-only Makerspace event before or after school. Make it short and sweet—10 or 15 minutes. Provide refreshments and they will come. They can better excite their students, if they have experienced the space. Give them special Makerspace passes for when they want to send students to visit the library for that explicit purpose. Depending upon how competitive your staff is, you could track usage by class and announce the biggest users on your school announcements. You could make signs for teachers to hang on their doors that say, "We use the Makerspaces." If you have a Library Advisory Council, they could help choose some of your Makerspaces. You know what will work best with your faculty to encourage and excite them.

Now, let's think about how students will find out about this new adventure.

Announce it at a back-to-school orientation or create a big reveal. If you are opening them at the beginning of the school year, point them out during your first meetings with students. Explain the procedures. Create excitement over the new opportunity. If you start them during the school year, do a big reveal. Cover the area up for a week before you want to start. Take guesses for what might be underneath the cover. Unveil them and watch the excitement flow.

Whether your school announcements are done over the intercom or in a student TV studio, use them to show and tell about the Makerspaces. If you have the capability of showing videos, then have a student capture some of the exciting activities happening at your Makerspaces. If your announcements are over an intercom, then ask if two students can talk about their experiences using them. Having two people share instead of one is likely to keep the audience interested longer. Having students write their script about Makerspaces is using some of the language arts skills in a real-world scenario.

Now how do we get the word to parents? Through multiple channels.

If your school has a newsletter, you want to have a regular column in it. Tell about your instruction, new materials, special events such as author visits and, of course, your Makerspaces. Start by explaining what they are and why you have them. Then give some specific examples. Invite families to stop when they are on campus. Advertise when you will have after-school Makerspace hours and explain the procedures. Include pictures. Truly, "a picture is worth a thousand words."

Phone blasts and e-mails can remind parents of your after-school hours events. It is also a great way to ask for items that they are going to throw away, such as paper towels and toilet paper tubes.

If your PTO/A has meetings, you want to attend them. If they have speakers, volunteer to be one of them. Share about Makerspaces. Offer to host one of the meetings in the Makerspace area. Seeing the spaces and participating in the activities, people are more likely to support and donate.

If you have a community newspaper that serves your area, get to know the reporter who writes the education beat. You have lots to share. If Makerspaces are a new concept in your community, then the paper will introduce the idea to a wide range of people that you might not reach with just a school publication.

Make a contact with the TV station that broadcasts in your area. They are always looking for local interest stories and your Makerspaces make a great visual presentation.

Whenever there are public events at your school, include Makerspaces. Do you have a curriculum night, back-to-school event, or STEAM fair? Encourage participants to visit your Makerspaces when they come for other events.

Start some opportunities that focus on Makerspaces. Experiment with different times. Some of them could be right after school, while others might be during evening hours. Start with just your school children. Have people sign up ahead of time so that you can plan for the numbers that will be in attendance. Children who have used the Makerspaces a lot during the day make excellent assistants for the after-hours events.

The 21st century allows us so many choices of social media: Facebook, Twitter, blogs, etc. Be sure you know your district's current policy on which ones are acceptable to use. Then use them. Yes, it is one more thing to do, but these are the 21st-century ways to communicate. If we want to be seen as educational leaders, and we do, then we have to walk the walk, not just talk about it.

If you have parent volunteers, see if one of them would like to handle some of the public relations for you. It is something they could do at home and still support the library. It would take something off your very full plate. I'm a real believer in delegating tasks whenever possible, because there aren't enough hours in the day to do everything you want to do. Makerspaces are great, but you have to plan some time in your life for them and then share the excitement and responsibility with others.

# CHAPTER 15

## Next Steps for Starting a Makerspace

When a new idea comes to the educational field, it is easy to get excited about it. You attend a conference session that addresses it or you read a book on the topic, then you want to give it a try. However, you go back to school and the daily tasks of a busy job get in the way of starting your new idea. Here are some thoughts to help you get started with Makerspaces and keep on track.

1.  First, plan to start small. Then, get your calendar out. Add the following tasks to it.

2.  Look at your physical space. Where can you put Makerspaces? You don't need to knock down walls, but you may want to move furniture around. What can you repurpose? Do you have the freedom to make changes to your walls? Can bulletin boards be put up? This is a great time to involve your Library Advisory Committee. They may see the space through different lens.

3.  Study your district's curriculum maps. Which content areas lend themselves to hands-on activities? Do you already own materials that you could use? How will it help students gain better understanding of the standard?

4.  Create one Makerspace by getting all the materials out and producing an "Ideas to Get Started Sheet." Decide if or how you will assess it. This step will take some time, but it will provide you with information that you will find useful when you want to use the materials in the future.

5.  Plan how you will tell others about it. Consider the audiences and what they need to know. Build excitement.

6.  Celebrate! Pat yourself on the back. You have started. Praise the teachers who send students. Congratulate parents who come to the after-school hours.

7. As you have time, repeat the process for other content areas. Add one Makerspace at a time, so you don't feel overwhelmed. Ask students and staff where their interests lie.

8. If you have volunteers, ask one of them to investigate grant possibilities. There are so many choices. One of them could meet your needs. They just need to know that you need funds.

9. Take a look at library finances and see where you might be able to have funds to use. Are there monies that could be moved from one account to another? Could you be allotted some science or school general account money?

10. Consider how you will store Makerspace materials. Be sure to label them. Do you want to store them by content area or months that you used them? Do you need a file cabinet? Use an Excel spreadsheet to keep track of various items that didn't come in their own sturdy box.

# Index

# About the Author

MARGE COX is currently the library media specialist at Veterans Memorial Elementary School in Naples, Florida. She began her educational career as a middle school home economics teacher. She received a Master of Library Science degree from Indiana University in 1985. Since that time, she has served as an elementary media services coordinator, media services director, weekly newspaper book review columnist, adjunct instructor, and coauthor of Libraries Unlimited's *The Media Specialist in the Writing Process* (2007). While residing in Indiana, she was active in the Indiana Reading Association, served as president of the Association of Indiana Media Educators (AIME), and won two awards from AIME: the Peggy L. Pfeiffer Service Award and the Danny Gunnells Intellectual Freedom Award. In 2015, while she was the library media specialist at Veterans Memorial Elementary School, the school won the Florida Power Library Award. In 2016, the Veterans Memorial Elementary School program was named School Library Program of the Year by American Association of School Librarians (AASL).